English in Action

Barbara H. Foley

Elizabeth R. Neblett

THOMSON
™
HEINLE

Australia • Canada • Mexico • Singapore • Spain • United Kingdom • United States

THOMSON

HEINLE

English in Action 1

by Barbara H. Foley and Elizabeth R. Neblett

Acquisition Editor: *Sherrise Roehr*
Director of Development: *James W. Brown*
Associate Developmental Editor: *Sarah Barnicle*
Editorial Assistant: *Elizabeth Allen*
Marketing Manager: *Eric Bredenberg*
Director, Global ESL Training & Development: *Evelyn Nelson*
Senior Production Editor: *Maryellen Killeen*
Senior Frontlist Buyer: *Mary Beth Hennebury*
Project Managers: *Anita Raducanu*
 Tünde A. Dewey

Compositor: *Pre-Press Co., Inc.*
Text Printer/Binder: *Courier Kendallville*
Text Designer: *Sue Gerald*
Cover Designer: *Gina Petti/Rotunda Design House*
Photo Researcher: *Claudine Corey*
Illustrators: *Scott MacNeill*
 Ray Medici
 Glen Giron, Roger Acaya, Ibarra
 Cristostomo, Leo Cultura of Raketshop
 Design Studio, Philippines

For permission to use material from this text or product contact us:
Tel: 1-800-730-2214
Fax: 1-800-730-2215
Web: www.thomsonrights.com

Library of Congress Cataloging-in-Publication Data

Foley, Barbara H.
 English in action I / Barbara H. Foley, Elizabeth R. Neblett.
 p. cm.
 The new grammar in action. ©1998.
 ISBN-13: 978-0-8384-2811-5
 ISBN-10: 0-8384-2811-8
 1. English language—Textbooks for foreign speakers.
 2. English language—Grammar—Problems, exercises, etc. I. Neblett, Elizabeth R. II. Foley, Barbara H. New grammar in action. III. Title.

 PE1128 .F559 2002
 428.2'4—dc21   2002017281

ASIA (excluding India)
Thomson Learning
60 Albert Street #15-01
Albert Complex
Singapore 189969

AUSTRALIA/NEW ZEALAND
Nelson/Thomson Learning
102 Dodds Street
South Melbourne
Victoria 3205 Australia

CANADA
Nelson/Thomson Learning
1120 Birchmount Road
Scarborough, Ontario
Canada M1K 5G4

LATIN AMERICA
Thomson Learning
Seneca, 53
Colonia Polanco
11560 México D.F. México

SPAIN
Thomson Learning
Calle Magallanes, 25
28015-Madrid
Espana

UK/EUROPE/MIDDLE EAST
Thomson Learning
Berkshire House
168-173 High Holborn
London, WC1V 7AA, United Kingdom

Acknowledgments

We would like to acknowledge the many individuals who helped, encouraged, and supported us during the writing and production of this series. In keeping with an open-ended format, we would like to offer a matching exercise. Please be advised, there is more than one correct "match" for each person. Thank you all!

Jim Brown	• for your creative eye for art and design.
Anita Raducanu	• for your enthusiasm and support.
Eric Bredenberg	• for your support, patience, and humor while guiding this project.
Sherrise Roehr	• for your faith in the authors.
Maryellen Killeen	• for your smiles and your stories.
Elizabeth Allen	• for your encouragement, comments, and suggestions.
Tünde A. Dewey	• for putting up with us!
All the Heinle sales reps	• for your understanding of the needs of teachers and programs.
The students at Union County College	• for your keeping us all on schedule.
The faculty and staff at UCC	• for your help with research
Our families	

The authors and publisher would like to thank the following reviewers and consultants:

Linda Boice
Elk Grove Unified School District, Sacramento, CA

Rocio Castiblanco
Seminole Community College, Sanford, FL

Jared Erfle
Antelope Valley High School, Lancaster, CA

Rob Kustusch
Triton Community College, River Grove, IL

Patricia Long
Old Marshall Adult School, Sacramento, CA

Kathleen Newton
New York City Board of Education, Bronx, NY

Alberto Panizo
Miami-Dade Community College, Miami, FL

Eric Rosenbaum
Bronx Community College, Bronx, NY

Michaela Safadi
South Gate Community, South Gate, CA

Armando Valdez
Huantes Learning and Leadership Development Center, San Antonio, TX

Contents

Contents

To the Teacher

Many years ago, I attended an ESL workshop in which the presenter asked a full audience, "How many of you read the **To the Teacher** at the front of the text?" Two participants raised their hands. Since that time, I have begged my publishers to release me from this responsibility, but have always been overruled.

As a teacher, you can form a clear first impression of this book. Flip through the pages. Will the format appeal to your students? Look carefully through the table of contents. Are most of the structures and contexts that your program has established included in the text? Thumb carefully through a few units. Will the activities and exercises, the support, the pace be appropriate for your students? If you wish, you can even read the rest of **To the Teacher** below.

English in Action is a four-level core language series for ESL/EFL students. It is a comprehensive revision and expansion of *The New Grammar in Action*. The popularity of the original edition delighted us, but we heard the same requests over and over: "Please include more readings and pronunciation," and "Could you add a workbook?" In planning the revision, our publisher threw budgetary concerns to the wind and decided to produce a four color, redesigned version. The revision also allowed us, the authors, an opportunity to refine the text. We are writers, but we are also teachers. We wrote a unit, then immediately tried it out in the classroom. Activities, tasks, and exercises were added, deleted, and changed in an on-going process. Students provided daily and honest feedback.

This first book is designed for students who have had little exposure to English, including new arrivals or adults who have lived in the United States for many years, but never formally studied English. The text assumes that students are literate in their native language.

The units in Book 1 branch from self, to school, family, home, jobs, and community. The contexts are everyday places and situations. The units build gradually, giving students the vocabulary, the grammar, and the expressions to talk about the situations and themselves. Students see, hear, and practice the language of everyday life in a great variety of exercises and activities. Because this is the first book and students are unsure of themselves, there is ever-present support in the form of grammar notes, examples, vocabulary boxes, and so on. By the end of Book 1, students should feel comfortable talking, reading, and writing about their lives using basic English phrases and sentences.

Each unit will take between five and seven hours of classroom time. If you have less time, you may need to choose the exercises you feel are the most appropriate for your students. You can assign some of the activities for homework. For example, after previewing **Writing Our Stories,** students can write their own stories at home, instead of in class. The short descriptions that follow give you an idea of the sections in each unit.

Finally, the book comes with an audio component. You need the audio program! The listening activities in the units are motivating and interesting. They provide other voices than that of the teacher. We have encouraged our adult students to buy the book/audio package. They tell us that they listen to the audio at home and in the car.

Dictionary

Each unit opens with a one- or two-page illustrated **Dictionary.** Students are asked to listen and repeat each item. All teachers realize that one repetition of vocabulary words does not produce mastery. Ask students to sit in groups and study the words together. Stage spelling bees. Play word bingo. Look for the same items in the classroom or school environment. Students must also study the words at home.

Active Grammar

Three to six pages of structured exercises present and practice the grammar of the unit. This first book integrates the new vocabulary and the grammar throughout all the activities in the unit. At this level, grammar mastery is not the goal, but rather an introduction to the basic structures of English and a feeling of comfort and security in the new language. As students progress through this section, they will find a variety of supportive features. Artwork and photos illustrate the context clearly. Answer boxes show the verbs or nouns to use in the answers. For many of the exercises, the entire class will be working together with your direction and explanations. Other exercises have a pairwork icon 👥 — students can try these with a partner. You can walk around the classroom, listening to students and answering their questions.

Pronunciation

Within the **Active Grammar** section is an exercise that focuses on pronunciation. These are specific pronunciation points that complement the grammar or vocabulary of the lesson, such as plural *s*, contractions, numbers, and syllables.

Working Together

For these one to two pages, students work in groups, trying out their new language with cooperative tasks, such as writing directions to the local hospital, interviewing partners, writing conversations, or arranging a person's daily schedule. Be prepared—students will make lots of mistakes during the practice. This exploration of the language is an important step in gaining comfort and fluency in English. If your students represent several different languages, group students with classmates who speak a language other than their own.

The Big Picture

This is our favorite section. It integrates listening, vocabulary, and structure. A large, lively picture shows a particular setting, such as a restaurant, a doctor's office, or an electronics store. Students listen to a short story or conversation, and then answer questions about the story, fill in exercises, review structures, or write conversations.

Reading

A short reading expands the context of the lesson. We did not manipulate a selection so that every sentence fits into the structure presented in the unit! There are new vocabulary words and structures. Teachers can help ESL readers learn that understanding the main idea is primary. They can then go back over the material to find the details that are interesting or relevant. If students can find the information they need, it is not necessary to master or look up every word.

Writing Our Stories

In this writing section, students first read a paragraph written by an ESL student or teacher. By using checklists or fill-in sentences, students are directed to brainstorm about their own schools, families, jobs, etc. Students then have an opportunity to write about themselves. Several teachers have told us about the creative ways they share student writing, including publishing student magazines, designing a class Web page, and displaying stories and photos taken by their students.

Practicing on Your Own

This is simple: it's a homework section. Some teachers ask students to do the exercises in class. Another suggestion for homework is the audio component. Ask students to listen to it three or four more times, reviewing the vocabulary and the exercises they did in class. Our students tell us that they often write the story from the Big Picture as a dictation activity.

Looking at . . . .

We can't claim any pedagogical theory for this section. We found it a convenient place for forms, math problems, or interesting information we located about the topic as we were writing the units.

Grammar Summary

Some teachers wanted this summary at the beginning of the unit; others were pleased to see it at the end. Use this section if and when you wish. Some students like to see the grammar up front, having a clear map of the developing grammar. We have found, though, that many of our students at this beginning level are confused with a clump of grammar explanations at the beginning of a unit. There are small grammar charts as needed throughout the unit. The ending summary brings them together.

I am sure we will be revising the text again in three or four years. We will be gathering your input during that time. You can always e-mail us at www.heinle.com with your comments, complaints, and suggestions.

About the Authors

Liz and I both work at Union County College in Elizabeth, New Jersey. We teach at the Institute for Intensive English, a large English as a Second Language program. Students from over 70 different countries study in our classes. Between us, Liz and I have been teaching at the college for over 40 years! When Liz isn't writing, she spends her time traveling, taking pictures, and watching her favorite baseball team, the New York Mets. Liz took many of the pictures in the texts, for which our students eagerly posed. In the warm weather, I can't start my day without a 15- or 20-mile bicycle ride. My idea of a good time always involves the outdoors: hiking, kayaking, or simply working in my garden.

Barbara H. Foley
Elizabeth R. Neblett

Photo Credits

All photos courtesy of Elizabeth R. Neblett with the following exceptions:

p.33 Courtesy of Anita Raducana, Tony Arruuza/CORBIS, Owen Franken/CORBIS, Bohemian Nomad Picturemakers/CORBIS;

p.79 Amos Nachoum/CORBIS; p.81 Gail Mooney/ CORBIS;

p.84 Mike Segar/Reuters New Media/CORBIS, Kelly-Mooney/CORBIS, Mark E. Gibson/CORBIS;

p.86 Dan Larmont/Corbis;

p.120 Pablo Corral/CORBIS, Jules T. Allen/CORBIS, Steve Raymer/CORBIS, Leif Skoogfors/ CORBIS, Dave Bartruff/CORBIS, Owen Franken/CORBIS, Jacques M. Chenet/CORBIS, Bob Rowan/Progressive Image/CORBIS, Roger Ressmeyer/CORBIS;

p.121 Catherine Karnow/CORBIS, Kelly-Mooney/CORBIS, Mark E. Gibson at CLM/CORBIS OUTLINE;

p.126 Owen Franken/CORBIS;

p.127 Richard T. Nowitz/CORBIS, Catherine Karnow/CORBIS;

p.132 Pablo Corral V/CORBIS, Willie Hill Jr./Index Stock Imagery;

p.141 SW Production/Index Stock Imagery;

p.144 Duomo/CORBIS, Layne Kennedy/CORBIS, Index Stock Imagery, Bill Bachmahn/Index Stock Imagery;

p.154 Doug Mazell/Index Stock Imagery;

p.194 Reuters New Media Inc./CORBIS;

p.210 Wallace Garrison/Index Stock Imagery;

p.211 Spike and Ethel/Index Stock Imagery;

p.227 Anthony James/ Index Stock Imagery.

Hello

Dictionary: One to Ten

A. Listen and repeat.

one student

two students

three students

four students

five students

six students

seven students

eight students

nine students

ten students

Active Grammar: Present Tense: *Be*

A. Listen.

B. Pair practice.

    A: Hello. My name is _____.

    B: Hi. I'm _____.

    A: Nice to meet you.

    B: Nice to meet you, too.

> I am = I'm

C. Complete.

    My first name is _____.

    My last name is _____.

Ana Santos
First name: Ana
Last name: Santos

 The Alphabet

 A. Listen.

Aa	Bb	Cc	Dd	Ee	Ff	Gg
Hh	Ii	Jj	Kk	Ll	Mm	Nn
Oo	Pp	Qq	Rr	Ss	Tt	Uu
Vv	Ww	Xx	Yy	Zz		

 B. Listen again and repeat.

C. Write.

> A = capital letter
> a = lowercase letter

Aa   Bb   Cc   Dd

Ee   Ff   Gg   Hh

Ii   Jj   Kk   Ll

Mm   Nn   Oo   Pp

Qq   Rr   Ss   Tt

Uu   Vv   Ww   Xx

Yy   Zz

 Please spell that.

A. Read.

A: What's your first name?

B: Ana.

A: What's your last name?

B: Santos.

A: Please spell that.

B: S – A – N – T – O – S.

B. Ask five students. Complete.

What's your first name?

What's your last name?

Carlos.

Moreno.

What's your first name?	What's your last name?
Carlos	Moreno
1.	
2.	
3.	
4.	
5.	

☀ My Classmates

A. Read.

My name is Sandra.

His name is Tuan.

Her name is Erica.

B. Say your classmates' names.

His name is Boris.

Her name is Jessica.

☀ Where are you from?

A. Complete.

What's your name?   My name is _____.

Where are you from?   I'm from _____.

B. Read.

What's her name?
Her name is Ana.
Where is she from?
She is from Mexico.

What's his name?
His name is Luis.
Where is he from?
He is from Colombia.

C. Match.

1. What's his name?   Her name is Roya.

2. Where is he from?   His name is Carlos.

3. What's her name?   She is from India.

4. Where is she from?   He is from Colombia.

 D. Pair practice. Ask about each person's name and country.

1.

   Monica

2.

   Moses

3.

   Yumi

4.

   Ela

5.

   Tuan

6.

   Martin

 E. Pronunciation: Contractions. Listen and repeat.

1. He is from Mexico.   He's from Mexico.

2. She is from Vietnam.   She's from Vietnam.

3. I am from Russia.   I'm from Russia.

4. He is from China.   He's from China.

5. I am from Haiti.   I'm from Haiti.

6. She is from Peru.   She's from Peru.

7. He is from Cuba.   He's from Cuba.

8. She is from Egypt.   She's from Egypt.

 F. Listen to Exercise E again. (Circle) the sentence you hear.

Numbers 1–20

A. Listen.

0	1	2	3	4	5	6	7	8	9	10
	11	12	13	14	15	16	17	18	19	20

B. Listen and repeat.

C. Write.

a. ten   _10_

b. six   _____

c. eleven   _____

d. three   _____

e. zero   _____

f. four   _____

g. twelve   _____

h. eighteen   _____

i. twenty   _____

j. seven   _____

k. fourteen   _____

l. nineteen   _____

D. Listen and circle.

a. 0   (1)   3

b. 3   4   8

c. 2   3   10

d. 0   1   11

e. 3   5   7

f. 4   14   15

g. 10   20   12

h. 6   7   17

i. 3   13   15

j. 2   3   13

k. 11   12   13

l. 8   18   19

☀ What's your telephone number?

A. Read.

A: What's your name?

B: Ana Santos.

A: And your telephone number?

B: 301-555-1796.

A: 301-555-1796?

B: Yes.

A: Thank you.

Culture Note
In a telephone number, say each number separately.

 B. Listen and write.

a. <u>5</u> <u>5</u> <u>5</u> . <u>3</u> <u>2</u> <u>3</u> <u>1</u>

b. _ _ _ - _ _ _ _

c. _ _ _ - _ _ _ _

d. _ _ _ - _ _ _ _

e. _ _ _ - _ _ _ - _ _ _ _

f. _ _ _ - _ _ _ - _ _ _ _

g. _ _ _ - _ _ _ - _ _ _ _

h. _ _ _ - _ _ _ - _ _ _ _

C. Pair practice. Say these telephone numbers with a partner.

a. 555-8320

b. 555-2390

c. 555-5636

d. 555-8124

e. 908-555-9932

f. 201-555-3452

g. 617-555-9898

h. 212-555-7335

Working Together

A. Ask five students these questions. Complete.

Helpful Expressions

Please repeat.
Please spell that.

What's your name?

Carlos.

Where are you from?

I am from Colombia.

Name	Country
Carlos	Colombia
1.	
2.	
3.	
4.	
5.	

B. Write about the students in Exercise A.

1. _____Carlos_____ is from _____Colombia_____.

2. _____ is from _____.

3. _____ is from _____.

4. _____ is from _____.

5. _____ is from _____.

6. _____ is from _____.

The Big Picture: My Classmates

A. Listen.

Peru	Hong Kong	Mexico	Japan	Haiti
Tomas	Jenny	Erica	Hiro	Marie

B. Listen again and write the correct name on each person.

Tomas	Hiro	Erica	Marie	Jenny

C. Complete with _He_ or _She_ and the name of the country.

1. This is Jenny. _____She_____ is from _____Hong Kong_____.

2. This is Erica. _____ is from _____.

3. This is Hiro. _____ is from _____.

4. This is Marie. _____ is from _____.

5. This is _____. _____ is from _____.

D. Listen. Write the number next to the answer.

___4___ He is from Japan.

___2___ I'm from Peru.

___3___ His name is Hiro.

___5___ Her name is Marie.

___1___ My name is Tomas.

___6___ She's from Haiti.

Reading: English

A. Before You Read. Circle the countries where most people speak English.

The United States   Britain   China

Colombia   Vietnam   Ireland

Australia   Russia   Japan

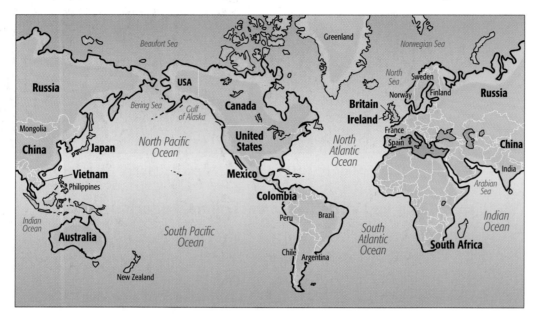

    People in the United States speak English. People in Canada, Britain, Australia, and Ireland speak English. Almost 500,000,000 people speak English.

    You can speak some English, too. You know words like *car, man, woman,* and *money.* You know sentences like *I'm a student* and *I'm from Mexico.*

    For you, English is a new language with new words and new grammar. It will take time to learn. Many people speak English. You will, too.

B. Write four words you know. Write four sentences you know.

Words	Sentences
telephone	Nice to meet you.

Writing Our Stories: All About Me

A. Read.

My name is Antonio.
I am from Mexico.
I am studying English.
I am a student at
Bayside Adult School.
My teacher is
Ms. Johnson.

B. Write.

My name is _____. I am from

_____. I am studying English. I am a student at

_____. My teacher is _____.

Practicing on Your Own

A. Complete.

1. His first name is _____ *Tuan* _____.

2. His middle initial is _____.

3. _____ last name is _____.

4. Her first name is _____.

5. Her middle initial is _____.

6. _____ last name is _____.

7. _____ student ID number is _____.

8. Luisa is a student at _____.

B. Match.

1. What's his name?   Her name is Imelda.

2. Where is he from?   He is from Mexico.

3. What's her name?   His name is Hector.

4. Where is she from?   I'm from Poland.

5. What's your name?   She is from the Philippines.

6. Where are you from?   My name is Dorota.

C. Complete.

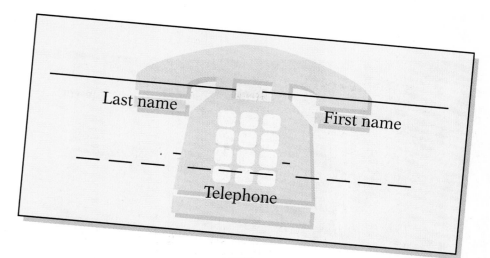

Last name

First name

Telephone

Name: _____
      first
      _____
      last

Telephone: (___) - ____ - _____

Last name

First name

Telephone

Name: _____
      first   initial

      last

Telephone:

(____) - ____ - _____

 Good-bye

 A. Listen.

 B. Pair practice.

       A: Good-bye, _____.

       B: Good-bye, _____.

       A: See you tomorrow.

       B: Have a nice day.

Learning Tip

> When I don't understand, I say, "Excuse me?"
> or I say, "I don't understand."

☐ I like this idea.
☐ I don't like this idea.
☐ I'm going to try this idea.

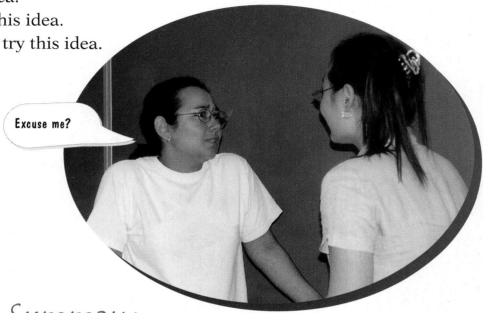

Excuse me?

Grammar Summary

▶ **1. Statements: be**	**Contractions**
I **am** a student.	I**'m** a student.
He **is** a student.	He**'s** a student.
She **is** a student.	She**'s** a student.
▶ **2. Possessive adjectives**	
My name is Ana.	
His name is Dan.	
Her name is Maria.	
▶ **3. *Wh-* questions**	
What's your name?	My name is Carlos.
Where are you from?	I'm from Colombia.

Hello **17**

2 The Classroom

Dictionary: Classroom Objects

A. Listen and repeat.

wall   clock   map

chalkboard

piece of chalk   window

eraser   door

teacher   pencil sharpener

desk   student

computer

chair

table

B. Listen and repeat.

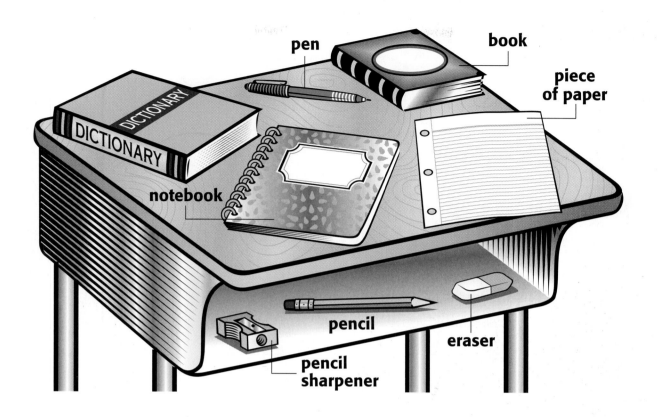

pen

book

piece
of paper

DICTIONARY

notebook

pencil
sharpener

pencil

eraser

**C. Check (✔) the items in *your* classroom.
Add to this list.**

a/an
Use **a** or **an** for the singular.
a book   an eraser

_____ a table

_____ a chair

_____ desks

_____ a map of the United States

_____ a map of the world

_____ a clock

_____ a computer

_____ a pencil sharpener

_____ a board

_____ a piece of chalk

_____ an eraser

_____ _____

_____ _____

_____ _____

Active Grammar: *Yes/No Questions*

 A. Listen. Number the conversations.

1.

2.

3.

_____   1   _____

> Is this your book?
> Yes, it is.
> No, it isn't.

 B. Listen and complete.

1. Is this your _____dictionary_____?

   Yes, it is. Thank you.

2. Is this your _____?

   Yes, it is. Thank you.

3. Is this your _____?

   No, it isn't.

4. Is this your _____?

   Yes, _____ _____. Thank you.

5. Is this your _____?

   No, _____ _____.

> pen
> paper
> ✓ dictionary
> notebook
> pencil sharpener

C. Pair practice.

 Is this your _____? Yes it is. Thank you.

 Is this your _____? No, it isn't.

1.   2.   3.  4.

Singular and Plural Nouns

A. Listen and repeat.

1.

a book   books

2.

a pencil   pencils

3.

a student   students

4.

a man   men

5.

a woman   women

6.

a child   children

B. Circle.

1.

a table   (tables)

2.

a clock   clocks

3.

an eraser   erasers

4.

a student   students

5.

a woman   women

6.

a man   men

A pencil—pencils

 A. Pronunciation: Plural nouns. Listen and circle.

1. (a pencil)   pencils
2. a student   students
3. a teacher   teachers
4. a man   men
5. a map   maps

6. a dictionary   dictionaries
7. an eraser   erasers
8. a notebook   notebooks
9. a classroom   classrooms
10. a woman   women

Sit with a partner. Say the words above.

B. Write.

1.

_____

5.

_____

2.

_____

6.

_____

3.

_____

7.

_____

4.

_____

8.

_____

Numbers 1–1000

A. Listen and repeat.

1 one	2 two	3 three	4 four	5 five	6 six	7 seven	8 eight	9 nine	10 ten
11 eleven	12 twelve	13 thirteen	14 fourteen	15 fifteen	16 sixteen	17 seventeen	18 eighteen	19 nineteen	20 twenty
21 twenty-one	22 twenty-two	23 twenty-three	24 twenty-four	25 twenty-five	26 twenty-six	27 twenty-seven	28 twenty-eight	29 twenty-nine	30 thirty

10 ten	20 twenty	30 thirty	40 forty	50 fifty	60 sixty	70 seventy	80 eighty	90 ninety	100 one hundred	1,000 one thousand

B. Listen and circle.

a. 4 15 (17)

b. 7 17 27

c. 14 15 16

d. 8 9 18

e. 22 27 29

f. 24 25 26

g. 13 23 33

h. 11 12 20

i. 43 44 45

j. 56 66 76

k. 62 67 76

l. 84 94 89

C. Write the number.

a. 6 _____six_____

b. 13 _____

c. 18 _____

d. 24 _____

e. 27 _____

f. 37 _____

g. 52 _____

h. 70 _____

i. 85 _____

j. 99 _____

There is—There are

A. Listen. Then talk about the desk.

B. Look at the desk above. Complete.

1. There is a _____ on the desk.

2. There is a piece of _____ on the desk.

3. There is an _____ on the desk.

4. There are two _____ on the desk.

5. There are three _____ on the desk.

6. There are five _____ on the desk.

7. There isn't a _____ on the desk.

C. Complete about *your* class. Use *is* or *are* and the number.

1. There _____ _____ teacher in our classroom.

2. There _____ _____ chairs in our classroom.

3. There _____ _____ desks in our classroom.

4. There _____ _____ pencil sharpener in our classroom.

5. There _____ _____ students in our class.

6. There _____ _____ men in our class.

7. There _____ _____ women in our class.

Working Together: My Classroom

A. Try this! Put two or three items from each student on a desk.

Student 1: Is this your cell phone?

Student 2: No, it isn't.

Student 1: Is this your cell phone?

Student 3: No, it isn't.

Student 1: Is this your cell phone?

Student 4: Yes, it is.

B. Interview two students. Circle their answers.

	Partner 1		Partner 2	
	_____		_____	
Do you have a dictionary?	Yes, I do.	No, I don't.	Yes, I do.	No, I don't.
Do you have an eraser?	Yes, I do.	No, I don't.	Yes, I do.	No, I don't.
Do you have a piece of paper?	Yes, I do.	No, I don't.	Yes, I do.	No, I don't.
Do you have a pencil sharpener?	Yes, I do.	No, I don't.	Yes, I do.	No, I don't.
Do you have a pen?	Yes, I do.	No, I don't.	Yes, I do.	No, I don't.
Do you have a pencil?	Yes, I do.	No, I don't.	Yes, I do.	No, I don't.

C. Draw a *large* picture of your classroom. Label everything!

A. Circle the things you see in this classroom.

a computer	a clock	a map of the United States
a board	a book	desks
a table	a door	a window
a pencil sharpener	a pencil	a man
a woman	a teacher	a child

 B. Listen.

C. Listen and circle.

1. Yes (No)
2. Yes   No
3. Yes   No
4. Yes   No
5. Yes   No

6. Yes   No
7. Yes   No
8. Yes   No
9. Yes   No
10. Yes   No

D. Complete. Write *is* or *are* and the number.

1. There ___are___ _____ten_____ students in this class.

2. There _____ _____ men and _____ women.

3. There _____ _____ teacher, Mr. Wilson.

4. There _____ _____ desks.

5. There _____ _____ maps on the wall.

6. There _____ _____ clock on the wall.

There is/There are		
There	is	one
	are	two
		three

E. Complete.

clock	clocks	student	students
map	✓maps	man	men
woman	women	desk	desks

1. There are two _____maps_____ on the wall.

2. There is a _____ of the world.

3. There are ten _____ in the class.

4. There are four _____ and six _____.

5. There is one _____ from India.

6. There are twelve _____ in the room.

7. There is a _____ on the wall.

A. Read these school signs. Ask your teacher about any signs you don't understand.

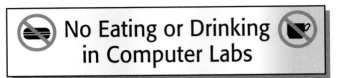

LIBRARY HOURS

Monday to Friday	9:00 A.M. to 10 P.M.
Saturday	9:00 A.M. to 5 P.M.
Sunday	1:00 P.M. to 5 P.M.

B. Walk around the school. Copy three signs that you see. Put your signs on the board.

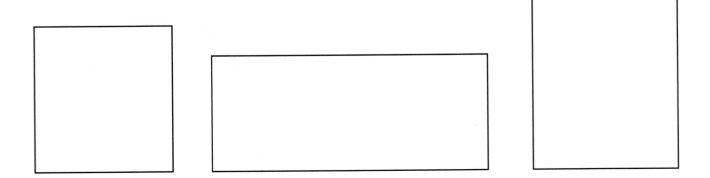

Writing Our Stories: My English Class

A. Read.

I study English at the English Adult School. My class is large. It's very large. There are 30 students in my class. We are from 20 different countries. We speak ten different languages.

Our classroom is small. There are 30 small desks. Our teacher, Mrs. Garcia, has a large desk for her books and her papers. We have many pencils, but we don't have a pencil sharpener. We are from many countries, but we don't have a map on the wall.

We need a larger classroom with a pencil sharpener and a map.

Writing Note
Use a period at the end of a sentence.

B. Write. Complete this story about your class.

I study English at _____.

There are _____ students in my class. We are from

_____ different countries. We speak _____ different languages.

Our classroom is _____. There are _____

_____

_____

_____

A. Write.

1. 10 _____ten_____   6. 22 _____
2. 14 _____   7. 35 _____
3. 18 _____   8. 47 _____
4. 19 _____   9. 69 _____
5. 20 _____   10. 100 _____

B. Complete.

1. Is this your pencil?   Yes, it ____is____.

2. Is this your dictionary? No, _____ _____.

3. Is this your computer?   Yes, _____ _____.

4. Is this your classroom?   Yes, _____ _____.

5. _____ this your notebook?   _____ _____ _____.

6. _____ _____ your _____? _____ _____ _____.

7. _____ _____ your _____? _____ _____ _____.

> Is this your book?
> Yes, it is.
> No, it isn't.

C. Complete with *There is* or *There are*.

1. _____There_____ _____are_____ twenty students in our class.

2. _____ _____ twelve students from my country.

3. _____ _____ one student from China.

4. _____ _____ a map of the world on the wall.

5. _____ _____ two doors in our classroom.

6. _____ _____ a large table in the classroom.

7. _____ _____ a computer on the table.

8. _____ _____ a chalkboard on the wall.

9. _____ _____ two erasers on the chalkboard.

Looking at Forms: School Registration

A. Complete.

SCHOOL REGISTRATION

Last Name: _____   First Name: _____
Student is registered for:

Class: _____   Room: _____

Teacher: _____   Date: _____

Grammar Summary

▶ **1.** *Yes / No* **questions**

Is this your book?   Yes, it **is**.   No, it **isn't**.

▶ **2. Singular and plural nouns**

Regular		*Irregular*	
book	book**s**	man	m**en**
map	map**s**	woman	wom**en**
student	student**s**	child	child**ren**

▶ **3.** *There is / There are*

There is a book on the table.

There are three books on the table.

3 The Family

Dictionary: The Family

A. Listen and repeat.

The Family

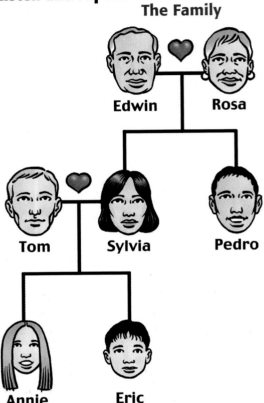

Edwin ♥ Rosa

Tom ♥ Sylvia   Pedro

Annie   Eric

husband
wife
father
mother
son
daughter
brother
sister
grandfather
grandmother
grandson
granddaughter
uncle
aunt
nephew
niece

father + mother = parents

B. Complete.

1. Eric and Annie: _____ brother and sister _____

2. Edwin and Rosa: _____

3. Rosa and Sylvia: _____

4. Edwin and Pedro: _____

5. Pedro and Eric: _____

6. Pedro and Annie: _____

7. Rosa and Annie: _____

8. Edwin and Eric: _____

Culture Note
Mom = mother
Dad = father

Active Grammar: *How old* Questions

A. Read.

How old is he?
He's 7.

Culture Note

We ask the ages of children and young people. We do not ask the age of an adult.

Margaret: This is my son, Nicholas.

Kathy: How old is he?

Margaret: He's 7. And this is my daughter, Alexa.

Kathy: How old is she?

Margaret: She's 3.

Kathy: You have a beautiful family.

B. Family photographs. Listen to the conversations. Number the photographs.

Relationship	Age
daughter	35
___	___

Relationship	Age
___	___
___	___

Relationship	Age
___	___
___	___

Listen again and write the relationships and ages.

Adjectives

A. Listen and repeat.

He's tall.

He's short.

She's heavy.

She's thin.

He's young.

He's old.

Her hair is long.
She has long hair.

Her hair is short.
She has short hair.

Her hair is straight.
She has straight hair.

Her hair is curly.
She has curly hair.

Her hair is wavy.
She has wavy hair.

He has a beard.

He has a moustache.

He's bald.

B. Complete about yourself.

1. I am **tall / short / medium height.**
2. I am **thin / heavy / average weight.**
3. I am **young / old / middle aged.**
4. My hair is _____.
   <u>color</u>
5. I have **short / long / medium-length** hair.
6. My hair is **straight / wavy / curly.**

blond

brown

black

red

gray

C. Describe.

1. Describe the president of the United States.
2. Describe a famous athlete.
3. Describe a movie actor or actress.

D. Answer.

| Yes, she is. No, she isn't. | Yes, it is. No, it isn't. |

1. Is she tall? _____
2. Is she heavy? _____
3. Is she old? _____
4. What color is her hair? Her hair is _____.
5. Is it curly? _____

| Yes, he is. No, he isn't. | Yes, it is. No, it isn't. |

6. Is he tall? _____
7. Is he thin? _____
8. Is he old? _____
9. What color is his hair? His hair is _____.
10. Is it long? _____

☀ What's your date of birth?

 A. Listen and repeat.

> **Months:** January, February, March, April, May, June,
> July, August, September, October, November, December
>
> **Days:** Sunday, Monday, Tuesday, Wednesday, Thursday, Friday, Saturday

B. Listen and repeat.

Sunday	Monday	Tuesday	Wednesday	Thursday	Friday	Saturday
		1 first	2 second	3 third	4 fourth	5 fifth
6 sixth	7 seventh	8 eighth	9 ninth	10 tenth	11 eleventh	12 twelfth
13 thirteenth	14 fourteenth	15 fifteenth	16 sixteenth	17 seventeenth	18 eighteenth	19 nineteenth
20 twentieth	21 twenty-first	22 twenty-second	23 twenty-third	24 twenty-fourth	25 twenty-fifth	26 twenty-sixth
27 twenty-seventh	28 twenty-eighth	29 twenty-ninth	30 thirtieth	31 thirty-first		

C. Listen. Write the date.

1. _____January 4, 2003_____
2. _____
3. _____
4. _____
5. _____
6. _____

7. _____
8. _____

Writing Note
Months begin with a capital letter.
January **F**ebruary

 Sit with a partner. Say the dates above.

D. Read and complete.

Date of birth: <u>9</u> / <u>14</u> / <u>75</u>
Month Day Year

Birth date: | | | | | |
Month   Day   Year

A: What's your date of birth?

B: September 14, 1975.

A: What's your birth date?

B: March 3, 1980.

Looking at Forms

married

single

divorced

A. Complete.

Name: _____ _____ _____
first   last   middle initial

Status: single married divorced   Sex: male female

Telephone: (   ) _____

Date of Birth: _____ _____ _____
month   day   year

NAME (Last, First, Middle)

MARITAL STATUS	SEX
Single Married Divorced	☐ Male ☐ Female
TELEPHONE NUMBER (include Area Code) ( )	BIRTH DATE Month / Day / Year _____/_____/_____

A. Draw your family tree. Complete this family tree. Show your parents, your husband or wife, your children, and your brothers and sisters. Add more circles if you need to. Write each person's name.

father _____   mother _____

you _____

 B. Explain your family tree to a partner.

Examples:

This is my mother. Her name is Manisha. She has five children.

This is my son. His name is Raj. He's six years old.

C. Family photographs. Bring in two or three photographs of your family. Tell your group about your family.

That's a nice picture. Is this you?

Your son is good-looking. He's tall!

Your son looks like you.

D. Write about a student in your class. Do not use the name. Write *he* or *she*.

_____

_____

_____

_____

_____

Read your description to the class. Can they guess the student?

E. Figure it out!

1. My daughter's son is my _____grandson_____.

2. My brother's daughter is my _____.

3. My brother's son is my _____.

4. My mother's brother is my _____.

5. My mother's sister is my _____.

*6. My daughter's husband is my _____.

*7. My sister's husband is my _____.

*8. My wife's father is my _____.

> *in-laws
>
> mother-in-law
> father-in-law
> sister-in-law
> brother-in-law
> son-in-law
> daughter-in-law

The Big Picture: A Family Photo

A. Look at the family photo. Write two adjectives for each person.

Bob: _tall, bald_

Sarah: _____

Linda: _____

Steve: _____

B. Listen. Write these names on the picture.

| Emily | Kim | Joanne | Mary | Andy |

C. Listen again. Write the ages that you hear.

D. Complete.

1. _____Mary_____ is tall and thin. She has short, curly hair.

2. _____ has a moustache, and he's bald.

3. _____ is five years old. She has long hair.

4. _____ is short and heavy. He has blond hair.

5. _____ is short and thin. She has short, straight hair.

6. _____ is tall and thin. He has wavy hair.

7. _____ is tall and heavy. She has short, curly hair.

E. Answer.

Andy

1. How old is Andy?

2. Is he short?

3. Is he heavy?

4. What color is his hair?

5. Is it curly?

Mary

1. How old is Mary?

2. Is she single?

3. Is she tall?

4. What color is her hair?

5. Is it long?

Ask and answer questions about other people in this family.

F. Pronunciation. Listen and repeat.

Statements
He is tall.
She is short.
It is curly.

Questions
Is he tall?
Is she short?
Is it curly?

Listen and complete. Then put a period (.) or a question mark (?) at the end of each sentence.

1. _____ _____ old

2. _____ _____ young

3. _____ _____ heavy

4. _____ _____ tall

5. _____ _____ thin

6. _____ _____ tall

7. _____ _____ short

8. _____ _____ heavy

 Practice the sentences above with a partner.

Reading: I Miss My Family

A. Before You Read.

1. Where do your brothers and sisters live? Where do your parents live?
2. Do you call them? Do you write them?

Donna

I have a computer. My brothers and my parents have computers, too. I e-mail everyone in my family. I write one e-mail and send it to everyone. We send photographs of the children, too!

Cecilia

My family is in the Philippines. My parents don't have a telephone. I write my parents once a month. I send them many photographs. They show the letters to my brothers and my sisters.

Gloria

I love to talk! I have a cell phone. My three sisters live in the United States, and I call them every week. My father lives in Colombia. I call him once a month. It's very expensive.

B. Check. (✓)

	Donna	Cecilia	Gloria
1. This person sends her family e-mail.	☐	☐	☐
2. This person sends photographs.	☐	☐	☐
3. This person calls her family a lot.	☐	☐	☐
4. This person has a computer.	☐	☐	☐
5. This person has a cell phone.	☐	☐	☐
6. This person writes letters.	☐	☐	☐

C. Discuss.

1. Do you have a computer? Do you e-mail anyone?
2. Do you write letters? Who do you write?
3. Do you have a cell phone? Do you call your family a lot?

A. Read.

My name is Liudmila. This is a photograph of my family. I am on the left. I have long, wavy hair. My eyes are brown. I am from Cuba. This is my husband, Carlos. He is 30 years old. Carlos is from Ecuador. He has black, curly hair. He is tall and handsome. He is hardworking. This is our son. His name is Jake. He is very active and friendly. He has brown hair and brown eyes. I think he looks like my husband.

B. Write about a photograph. Bring in a photograph of your family. Write about your photograph.

This is a picture of _____

_____

_____

_____

_____

_____

_____

_____

_____

Writing Note
A name begins with a capital letter.

Practicing on Your Own

A. Write the answer.

> No, she isn't. She's single. He lives in New Jersey. ✓ That's my brother. Her name is Erica. Yes, he's married.
>
> She's 23. She lives in Texas. His name is Shin Kim. He's 26. That's my sister.

1. Who's this? _____That's my brother._____
2. What's his name? _____
3. How old is he? _____
4. Where does he live? _____
5. Is he married? _____

6. Who's this? _____
7. What's her name? _____
8. How old is she? _____
9. Where does she live? _____
10. Is she married? _____

B. Write the date.

1. 1/3/03 _____January 3, 2003_____
2. 4/7/99 _____
3. 3/21/86 _____
4. 4/8/75 _____
5. 9/6/68 _____
6. 11/12/00 _____
7. 12/25/05 _____

Writing Note
Put a comma between the day and the year.
January 3, 2003

I study with two classmates. We work together two days a week after class.

☐ I like this idea.
☐ I don't like this idea.
☐ I'm going to try this idea.

Grammar Summary

▶ **1. *How old* questions**	
How old is he?	He's 15.
How old is she?	She's 7.
▶ **2. Adjectives**	
He's **tall.** He's **young.**	
He has **black** hair.	
▶ **3. Short questions and answers**	
Is he tall?	Yes, he **is.** No, he **isn't.**
Is she old?	Yes, she **is.** No, she **isn't.**
Is his hair long?	Yes, it **is.** No, it **isn't.**

Moving Day

 Dictionary: Rooms, Furniture, Locations

A. Listen and repeat.

Rooms

living room

dining room

kitchen

bathroom

bedroom

Furniture

sofa

armchair

TV

lamp

picture

bookcase

coffee table

end table

table

chair

rug

mirror

bed

dresser

desk

night table

stove

sink

microwave

refrigerator

sink

toilet

bathtub

shower

Locations

The book is on the chair.

The book is under the chair.

The book is next to the chair.

The book is between the chair and the desk.

The book is in the desk.

The picture is over the chair.

Active Grammar: Prepositions

A. Read.

A: Where do you want this armchair?

B: Put it in the living room.

A: Where do you want this lamp?

B: Put it in the bedroom.

B. Complete.

1. Put the refrigerator in the _____ kitchen _____.

2. Put the bed in the _____.

3. Put the coffee table in the _____.

4. Put the dresser in the _____.

5. Put the armchair in the _____.

6. Put the table in the _____.

7. Put the stove in the _____.

C. Complete these sentences about the house.

1. The mirror is _____ the bed.

2. The stereo is _____ the boxes.

3. The telephone is _____ the night table.

4. The pillows are _____ the dresser.

5. The computer is _____ the coffee table.

6. The night table is _____ the bed.

7. The end table is _____ the sofa.

8. The TV is _____ the desk.

9. The armchair is _____ the desk.

10. The cat is _____ the sofa.

11. The lamp is _____ the coffee table.

12. The boxes are _____ the window.

D. Ask and answer.

> Where is the TV?
> It's on the desk.

> Where are the books?
> They're next to the box.

1. Where is the computer?

2. Where is the mirror?

3. Where are the keys?

4. Where is the cell phone?

5. Where are the movers?

6. Where is the desk chair?

7. Where are the boxes?

8. Where is the rug?

☀ Where is my cell phone?

Yes, it is. No, it isn't.	Yes, they are. No, they aren't.

A. Answer.

1. Is the cell phone on the coffee table?

2. Are the photos on the coffee table?

3. Is the remote on the desk?

4. Are the keys next to the computer?

5. Are the pillows on the sofa?

6. Is the printer next to the computer?

7. Is the clock on the bookcase?

8. Is the cat under the sofa?

B. Look at the picture above and read the conversations.

Conversation 1

A: Where is my cell phone?

B: Is it on the coffee table?

A: No, it isn't.

B: Is it under the coffee table?

A: No, it isn't.

B: Is it on the floor?

A: Yes, here it is!

Conversation 2

A: Where are my glasses?

B: Are they next to the stereo?

A: No, they aren't.

B: Are they under the coffee table?

A: No, they aren't.

B: Are they on the armchair?

A: Yes, here they are!

C. Look at the picture above. Practice the conversations again with these items.

clock	pillows	house keys
camera	books	remote

A. Sharing an apartment. You and a partner are sharing an apartment. Place all of these items in your living room. Where is each item?

window	door
window	

the sofa

two chairs

the coffee table

the desk

the bookcase

the lamps

the end tables

the TV

the telephone

B. Look around your classroom. Write the locations of five items.

1. _____The clock is over the door._____

2. _____

3. _____

4. _____

5. _____

6. _____

A. Read.

South Avenue

A: What's your new address?

B: 419 South Avenue.

A: What town?

B: Cranford.

A: And what's your zip code?

B: 07016.

 B. Pronunciation: Street addresses. Listen and repeat.

a.

Main Street

b.

Maple Street

c.

Second Street

d.

Central Avenue

e.

Park Avenue

f.

North Avenue

 C. Listen. Write the addresses.

1. _____73_____ North Avenue

2. _____ Maple Street

3. _____ Central Avenue

4. _____ Park Avenue

5. _____ First Street

6. _____ Main Street

👥 **Repeat the addresses above with a partner.**

 Sending a letter

A. Interview three students.

What's your name?	What's your address?	What's your zip code?
Pierre	349 Pine Place Santa Rosa	03402
1.		
2.		
3.		

B. Read.

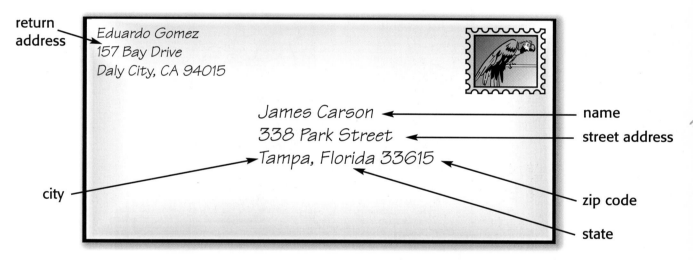

return address

Eduardo Gomez
157 Bay Drive
Daly City, CA 94015

James Carson → name
338 Park Street → street address
Tampa, Florida 33615 → zip code

city

state

C. Address this envelope to a friend.

The Big Picture: A Dorm Room

A. Write the name of each item on the picture.

bed	CDs	dresser	computer	small table	printer
pillows	clothes	desk	remote	stereo	telephone

 B. Listen to this conversation between Kathy and her father.

1. Is Kathy at home?
2. Where is Kathy?
3. Is her room large or small?

C. Complete.

1. The TV is _____ the night table.

2. The pillow is _____ the window.

3. The stereo is _____ the dresser.

4. The CDs are _____ the stereo.

5. The computer is _____ the desk.

6. The printer is _____ the computer.

7. Some clothes are _____ the closet.

8. Some clothes are _____ the floor.

9. The telephone is _____ the bed.

10. Kathy is _____ her dorm room.

D. Sit with a partner. Ask and answer these questions.

Yes, it is.
No, it isn't.

Yes, they are.
No, they aren't.

1. Is the bed on the right?
2. Is the dresser on the left?
3. Is the telephone under the bed?
4. Is the bookcase on the desk?
5. Is the stereo next to the computer?

6. Is the TV on the dresser?
7. Are the CDs next to the TV?
8. Are the clothes on the bed?
9. Is the remote on the TV?
10. Are the pillows on the bed?

E. Ask and answer questions about these items in Kathy's room.

Where is the stereo?
It's on the dresser.

Where are the CDs?
They're next to the stereo.

the computer
the telephone
her boots
the remote

the books
the TV
the shoes
the telephone

Reading: Classified Ads

A. Before You Read. What is the name of your local paper? Where is the classified ad section?

Garage Sales

In your local newspaper, you can find ads for garage sales, yard sales, or tag sales in your area. At these sales you can buy furniture, electronic equipment, children's toys and clothing, kitchen items, etc. at very good prices.

1	**Clark** – 16 Poplar Drive – Saturday 9am–3pm. Sofa, child's bedroom set, kitchen table, kitchen items, tools. Rain or shine.	5	**Fanwood** – 33 West End Avenue – Three Family Garage Sale. Saturday 9–4. Dishes, kitchen items, books, clothing, exercise equipment, refrigerator.
2	**Clark** – 32 Standish Way – Friday and Saturday 10am–5pm. Baby items, car seat, playpen, crib, stroller, lots of toys and clothing.	6	**Garwood** – 472 Summit Avenue – Friday and Saturday 9–3. Moving Sale. Twin beds, 2 sofas, washing machine and dryer, bookcase, chairs, coffee table, lamps, and much more!
3	**Cranford** – 55 Holly Street – Moving to Florida! Saturday 8am–6pm. Lots of furniture! Beds, chairs, sofas, end tables, night tables, dining room set, T.V.	7	**Plainfield** – 377 Raritan Road – Saturday Neighborhood Garage Sale – Furniture, kitchen items, small appliances, rugs, lamps, tools, stereo, CDs.
4	**Cranford** – 456 Willow Street – Friday 9 to 5. Something for everyone! Tools, garden equipment, furniture, misc.	8	**Summit** – 44 North Avenue – Friday and Saturday 9–3. Pool table, two bicycles, sports equipment, toys, and games.

B. Scan these ads. Write the number of one or two garage sale ads.

1. This sale has baby items. _____2_____

2. This sale has tools. _____

3. This sale has a TV. _____

4. This sale has a sofa. _____

5. This sale has kitchen items. _____

6. This sale has bicycles. _____

7. This sale has a refrigerator. _____

> What are you looking for? Which garage sale is good for you?

Writing Our Stories: At Home

A. Read.

I rent a room in a house in San Diego. My family is in Poland, and I live alone. I work all day, and I go to school at night. I don't want an apartment. I don't need a kitchen. I only eat breakfast at home. There is a small refrigerator and a micro-wave in the room. My TV is on a small table.

I live in a house in San Diego. It's all on one floor. The house has seven rooms. There are three bedrooms and two bathrooms. There is a family room, too. There is a TV and a computer in the family room. We need a large house. I have three children, and my mother lives with us, too.

B. Check the information that is true about you.

☐ I live in a house.
☐ I live in an apartment.
☐ I live alone.
☐ I live with _____.

☐ There are _____ rooms.
☐ I have a small _____.
☐ I have a large _____.
☐ There's a TV in my bedroom.

C. Write.

I live at _____ _____ in _____.
       number   street   city

I live in _____. I live with _____.
   a house / an apartment / a room

My home has _____ rooms. _____.

_____

_____

_____

_____

_____

Writing Note
Street names begin with capital letters: <u>N</u>orth <u>A</u>venue

A. Complete.

1. Where ____is____ the microwave? _____

2. Where _____ the glasses? _____

3. Where _____ the clock? _____

4. Where _____ the window? _____

5. Where _____ the cups? _____

6. Where _____ the table? _____

7. Where _____ the boxes? _____

8. Where _____ coffee maker? _____

B. Answer.

1. Is the pot on the stove? _____

2. Are the flowers on the table? _____

3. Is the window over the stove? _____

4. Are the cups on the counter? _____

5. Are the glasses in the sink? _____

6. Is the clock on the table? _____

7. Is the stove next to the refrigerator? _____

8. Are the boxes on the table? _____

Learning Tip

I make flash cards to study vocabulary.
On one side, I write the word in English.
On the other side, I write the word
in my language.

☐ I like this idea.
☐ I don't like this idea.
☐ I'm going to try this idea.

table

la mesa

Grammar Summary

> **1. Prepositions**

The sofa is **in** the living room.

The end table is **next to** the sofa.

The books are **on** the end table.

> **2. *Where* questions**

Where is the dresser?	It's next to the bed.
Where are the shoes?	They're under the bed.

> **3. *Yes / No* questions**

Is the telephone on the counter?	Yes, it **is.**	No, it **isn't.**
Are the CDs next to the stereo?	Yes, they **are.**	No, they **aren't.**

5 I'm Busy

 Dictionary: Actions

A. Listen and repeat.

He is eating.

She is washing the car.

She is listening to music.

They are studying.

He is cooking.

She is sleeping.

He is reading.

She is drinking.

They are talking.

They are watching TV.

He is doing his homework.

She is cleaning the house.

She is driving.

They are walking.

She is making lunch.

He is doing the laundry.

B. Complete.

1. He ____is talking____ on the telephone.

2. She _____ the newspaper.

3. I _____ in my book.

4. They _____ a movie.

5. The students _____ English.

6. He's in bed. He _____.

7. She _____ a cup of coffee.

8. They _____ to the stereo.

9. She _____ dinner.

10. He _____ a hamburger.

is reading
are studying
✓ is talking
am writing
are watching
is drinking
is cooking
is eating
is sleeping
are listening

C. Pronunciation: Contractions. Listen.

Long form	Contraction
She is reading.	She's reading.
He is sleeping.	He's sleeping.
I am studying.	I'm studying.
We are talking.	We're talking.
They are eating.	They're eating.
You are cooking.	You're cooking.

(Circle) the form you hear.

1. **a.** He is walking.   **b.** He's walking.

2. **a.** She is cleaning.   **b.** She's cleaning.

3. **a.** I am making lunch.   **b.** I'm making lunch.

4. **a.** You are driving.   **b.** You're driving.

5. **a.** They are watching TV.   **b.** They're watching TV.

6. **a.** We are studying.   **b.** We're studying.

Practice both forms of the sentences above with a partner.

Active Grammar: Present Continuous Statements

A. Read. Underline the verbs.

It is Saturday morning, and everyone in the Lee family is busy. Jenny is in the bathroom. She is taking a shower. Jenny is getting ready for work. David is in his bedroom. He is studying for a test on Monday. Mrs. Lee is in the living room. She is cleaning. Right now, she is vacuuming the rug. Mr. Lee is in the kitchen. He is cooking lunch for the family. Carla is helping. She is washing the dishes. Grandma Lee is in the kitchen, too. She is doing the laundry.

B. Match.

1. Where is Jenny?	She's in the living room.
2. What is she doing?	He's cooking lunch.
3. Where is Mrs. Lee?	He's studying.
4. What is she doing?	She's in the bathroom.
5. Where is Mr. Lee?	She's cleaning.
6. What is he doing?	She's taking a shower.
7. Where is David?	He's in the kitchen.
8. What is he doing?	He's in his bedroom.

C. Ask and answer.

1. Is Jenny sleeping?
2. Is she getting ready for work?
3. Is David in his bedroom?
4. Is he studying?
5. Is Mrs. Lee in the living room?
6. Is she watching TV?

7. Are Mr. Lee and Carla in the kitchen?
8. Are they cooking dinner?
9. Is Carla washing the dishes?
10. Are they talking?
11. Is Grandma in the kitchen?
12. Is Grandma doing the laundry?

D. Read.

David: Hello.

Mark: Hi. This is Mark. Can you talk now?

David: I can't. I'm studying for a test. Can I call you later?

Mark: Sure.

Culture Note
On the telephone, say:
This is (name).
Example: This is Maria.

E. Practice this conversation.

A: Hello.

B: Hi, _____. This is _____. Can you talk now?

A: No, I can't. I'm _____. Can I call you later?

B: Sure.

 My, Your, His, Her

Possessive Adjectives
I—my   He—his
You—your   She—her

A. Act out these classroom directions. What are you doing? What is he/she doing?

Luis, write your name on the board.

I'm writing my name.

He's writing his name.

1. Stand up.
2. Walk to the blackboard.
3. Write your last name on the board.
4. Erase your name.
5. Sit down.

6. Open your book.
7. Close your book.
8. Raise your hand.
9. Point to the clock.
10. Sharpen your pencil.

B. Complete.

1. I'm talking to ____my____ sister.
2. You're doing _____ homework.
3. He's opening _____ book.
4. She's writing _____ address.
5. I'm sharpening _____ pencil.
6. He's washing _____ car.
7. He's calling _____ father.
8. She's talking to _____ brother.
9. You're cleaning _____ bedroom.
10. She's washing _____ hands.

Working Together

A. Sit in a group and write a story about this family. Name each person. Where is each person? What is each person doing?

B. Choose two locations. What are people doing? Use your imagination.

park

cafeteria

student lounge

airplane

computer lab

bus

office

car

Example: car

1. A man is driving.

2. A woman is listening to the radio.

3. A driver is stopping at the red light.

4. A man is talking on his cell phone.

5. A woman is drinking a cup of coffee.

A. Listen to the conversation between Tommy and his mother.

B. Listen again and write the names on the picture.

Mom	Tommy	Brian	Katie	Dad

C. Complete.

1. Tommy is in the _____.

2. Brian is in the _____.

3. Katie _____ in her _____.

4. Dad _____ in the _____.

5. Mom _____ at _____.

D. Listen and answer.

1. __No, she isn't.__
2. _____
3. _____
4. _____
5. _____
6. _____
7. _____

Yes, he is.
No, he isn't.

Yes, she is.
No, she isn't.

E. Match.

1. Where is Tommy?   No, he isn't.
2. What is he doing?   He's in the kitchen.
3. Is Tommy playing video games?   He's playing video games.
4. Is Tommy talking to his mother?   He's watching TV.
5. Where is Brian?   No, he isn't.
6. What is he doing?   Yes, he is.
7. Is Brian sleeping?   He's in the living room.

F. Answer.

1. Where is Dad? __He's in the living room.__
2. Is he cooking dinner? _____
3. What's he doing? _____
4. Where is Katie? _____
5. What's she doing? _____
6. Is she doing her homework? _____

G. Write a story about this family in your notebook.

Reading: The Phone Book

A. Before You Read. Where is your phone book? What cities does it include?

Palmer David 177 Central Av Cranford......................555-1483	Pannullo T 46 Sussex St Plainfield.............................555-4316
Palmer Emily 43 Grand St Cranford...........................555-1234	Panosh John 336 Forest Ave Westfield.......................555-8274
Palmer R 34 Broad St Essex.......................................555-5477	Pantagis Stephen 3 Chester Ave Essex......................555-8682
Palmer William 6 Linden L Fanwood.........................555-6134	Pantagis Susan 200 Broad St Fanwood......................555-8833
Palmieri Ann 45 Grove St Fanwood............................555-5579	Pantano N 59 Maple St Plainfield..............................555-7604
Palmieri Fred 114 Maple T Essex...............................555-9966	Pantoja R 80 Prospect St Essex.................................555-9038
Palumbo Ed 110 South Ave Warrenville......................555-1024	Paoli P 621 Sunny Drive Plainfield.............................555-8652
Palumbo George 110 South Av Essex.........................555-6403	Paolo Stephen 56 Davis Rd Plainfield.........................555-0294
Palumbo Henry 184 Second St Essex..........................555-4403	Paone Joan 44 Harding St Essex.................................555-5657
Palumbo L 23 Coles Way Fanwood.............................555-7761	Papa's Pizza 77 Main St Plainfield..............................555-2534
Palumbo P 650 Brant Crt Cranford.............................555-7463	Papen Chris 204 Euclid Av Plainfield...........................555-8541
Palusci Ellen 67 Main St Warrenville..........................555-9832	Papen George 399 Glen Road Fanwood.......................555-2538
Palusci Martin 173 First St Essex................................555-4411	Papen Theresa 75 Glen Road Fanwood.......................555-7520
Panagos Cleaners 43 South Ave Essex........................555-7764	Papik B 34 Hazel Court Warrenville.............................555-6852
Panagos H 65 Rahway Rd Fanwood...........................555-0102	Pappas John and Marge 12 Lake Ave Essex...........555-6427
Panagos Joseph 76 Third Av Fanwood........................555-2310	Pappas S 216 State St Plainfield.................................555-0208
Panarese B 876 Park Av Warrenville............................555-8525	Parada Juan 169 Sunset St Plainfield..........................555-7314
Panarese Brad 9 Willow Ave Cranford........................555-0113	Parada Ricardo 14 Forest Ave Essex...........................555-6291
Panarese C 453 Rogers Way Essex..............................555-7509	Parada Teresa 90 South Av Cranford..........................555-7326
Panasik Craig 65 Davis Road Fanwood.......................555-8029	Paradise Ed 501 Martin St Fanwood...........................555-6491
Panek Darren 431 Coles Way Essex............................555-7435	Paradise H 36 Grant Av Essex....................................555-2509
Panek Katherine 107 Charles St Fanwood..................555-1128	Pardo Charles 153 Glen Road Fanwood......................555-8574
Panek Bakery 54 Center St Cranford..........................555-7039	Pardon R 54 Paulis St Warrenville..............................555-2530
Panera Richard 87 Route 22 Cranford........................555-2085	Parente A 591 Hort St Warrenville.............................555-0203
Pang Hang 43 Grove Av Fanwood.............................555-6965	Parente E 88 Broad St Westield.................................555-8637
Pang J 44 Thomas St Plainfield..................................555-7413	Parisi L 71 Francis Av Plainfield..................................555-8630
Pang Y 87 Woods Way Plainfield................................555-8530	Parisi M 490 Kent Place Plainfield...............................555-3250
Pango L 866 Baker St Plainfield..................................555-2527	Park In-Chui 937 North Av Fanwood..........................555-7831
Pannone 60 Davis Rd Fanwood.................................555-4682	Park Jeong 503 Lake Av Cranford..............................555-1509

A B C D E F G H I J K L M N O **P** Q R S T U V W X Y Z

B. Write the phone number.

Emily Palmer _____   John and Marge Pappas _____

Y Pang   _____   Henry Palumbo   _____

Juan Parada   _____   Charles Pardo   _____

C. Write the address.

Papa's Pizza   _____

Panagos Cleaners   _____

Jeong Park   _____

Writing Our Stories: What's Happening?

A. Read.

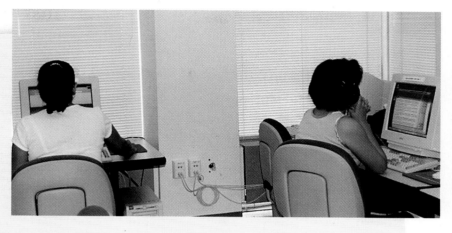

My name is Renata. I am studying English at Davis Community College. There are many students in this school. Right now, many students are studying in their classrooms. Some students are studying or reading in the library. Some students are using computers. Some students are eating in the cafeteria. Other students are talking, walking in the halls, or looking at books in the bookstore. This school is busy all the time.

B. Name four places in your school.

_____   _____

_____   _____

C. Write about your school. What is happening now?

My name is _____. I am a student at _____

_____. There are many students in this school. Right now,

many students _____ in their classrooms. Some

students _____ in the

_____. Some students

_____ in the

_____. Other students

_____. My school

is busy all the time.

> **Writing Note**
> The name of your school begins with a capital letter.

A. Complete this form.

Name: Orlando J. Gutierrez

Telephone Number: 666-555-4218

Student ID Number: 888-910-6160

Instructions

Use a number 2 pencil

Darken circles completely

Examples:

Wrong ✓

Wrong ✗

Wrong ◔

Right ●

Print your name in the boxes. Blacken the circle under each letter.

LAST NAME — GUTIERREZ

FIRST NAME — ORLANDO

MI — J

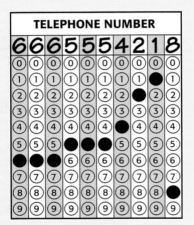

TELEPHONE NUMBER — 6665554218

STUDENT ID NUMBER — 888

B. Complete this form about yourself.

Name: ______________________________

Telephone Number: ______________________

Student ID Number: _____________________

Instructions

Use a number 2 pencil

Darken circles completely

Examples:

Wrong

Wrong

Wrong

Right

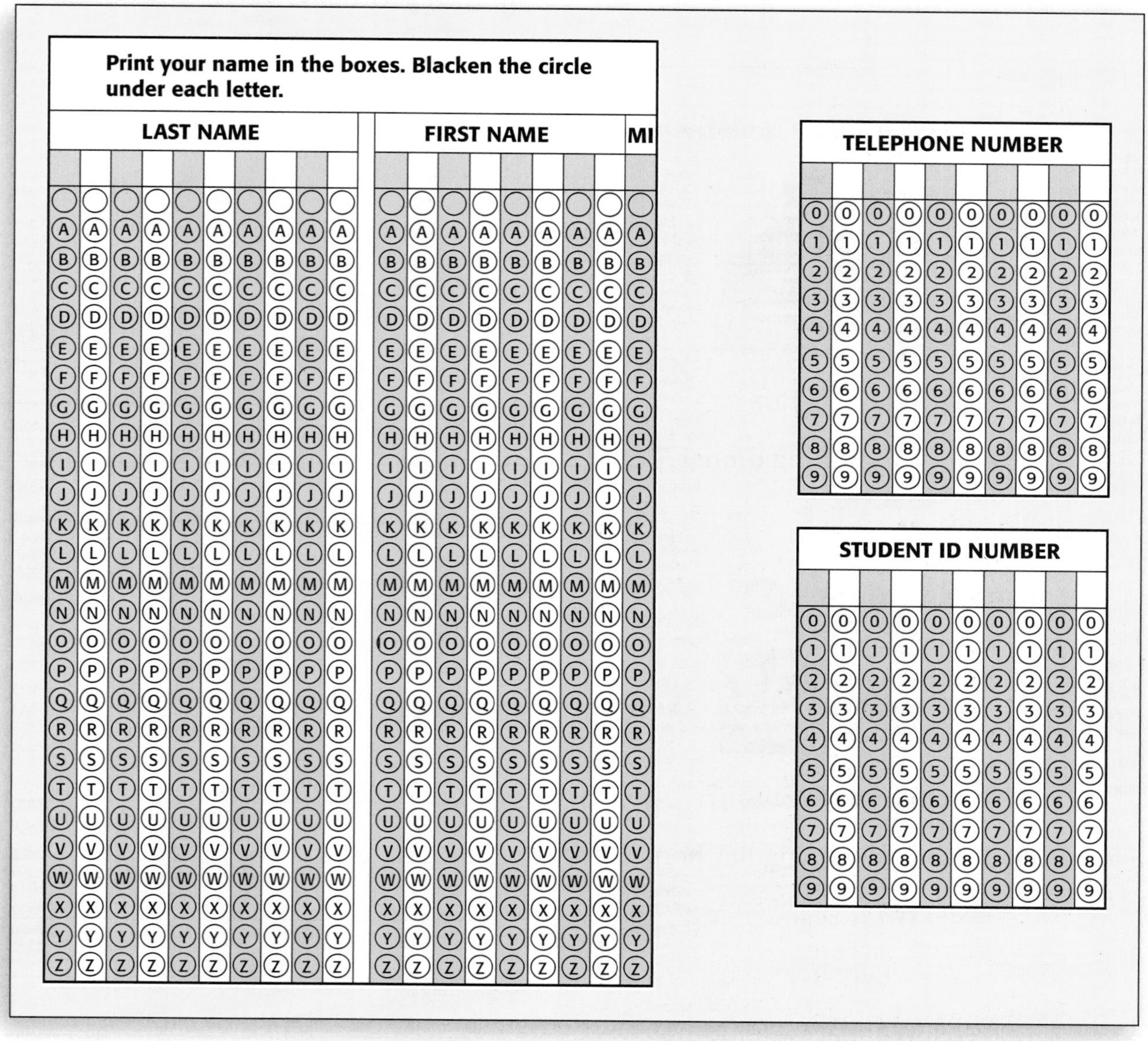
Print your name in the boxes. Blacken the circle under each letter.
LAST NAME
FIRST NAME
MI
TELEPHONE NUMBER
STUDENT ID NUMBER

Practicing on Your Own

A. Complete.

1. He ____is cooking____ in the kitchen.

2. She _____ in her bedroom.

3. She _____ in the bathroom.

4. I _____ in the dining room.

5. They _____ in the living room.

6. We _____ in the classroom.

7. I _____ in the library.

B. Answer these questions.

1. Where is Bob? _____

2. Is he eating dinner? _____

3. What is he doing? _____

4. Where is Susan? _____

5. Is she doing her homework? _____

6. What is she doing? _____

7. Where are you? _____

8. What are you doing? _____

9. Are you doing your homework? _____

Learning Tip

> **I watch TV in English. I watch easy programs.**
> **Sometimes I watch TV with my children.**

☐ I like this idea.
☐ I don't like this idea.
☐ I'm going to try this idea.

Grammar Summary

▶ **1. Present continuous statements**	

I **am studying.**	I**'m studying.**
He **is sleeping.**	He**'s sleeping.**
She **is eating.**	She**'s eating.**
They **are watching** TV.	They**'re watching** TV.

▶ **2. *Yes / No* questions**

Are you watching TV?	Yes, I **am.**	No, I**'m not.**
Is she watching TV?	Yes, she **is.**	No, she **isn't.**
Is he watching TV?	Yes, he **is.**	No, he **isn't.**
Are they watching TV?	Yes, they **are.**	No, they **aren't.**

▶ **3. *Wh-* questions**

Where is he?	He's in the kitchen.
What is he doing?	He's cooking.

6 My City

 A. Listen and repeat.

Adjectives

large

small

quiet

noisy

busy

clean

dirty

fun

safe

dangerous

beautiful

ugly

cheap

expensive

interesting

boring

heavy/light

hardworking

friendly

unfriendly

Location

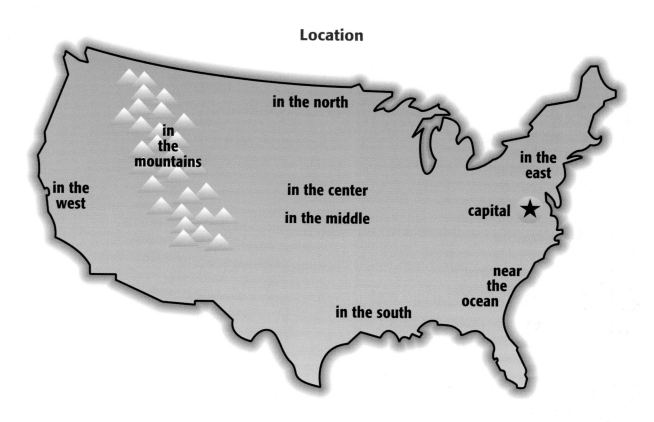

in the north

in the mountains

in the west

in the center

in the middle

in the east

capital ★

in the south

near the ocean

Climate

wet

dry

humid

hot

cold

Active Grammar: Adjective Review

A. Match the opposites.

1. busy
2. wet
3. clean
4. quiet
5. cheap
6. beautiful
7. interesting
8. small
9. friendly
10. heavy

a. ugly
b. expensive
c. unfriendly
d. boring
e. light
f. noisy
g. dry
h. quiet
i. dirty
j. large

B. Listen and complete with an adjective.

1. Miles City, Montana, is a _____small_____ city.

2. The movies in New York City are _____.

3. Downtown Chicago is _____.

4. The weather in Phoenix, Arizona, is _____ and _____.

5. The people in Atlanta, Georgia, are _____.

6. The streets in San Francisco, California, are _____.

7. The traffic in Boston, Massachusetts, is _____.

8. New Orleans, Louisiana, is an _____ city.

C. Can you label the U.S. map?

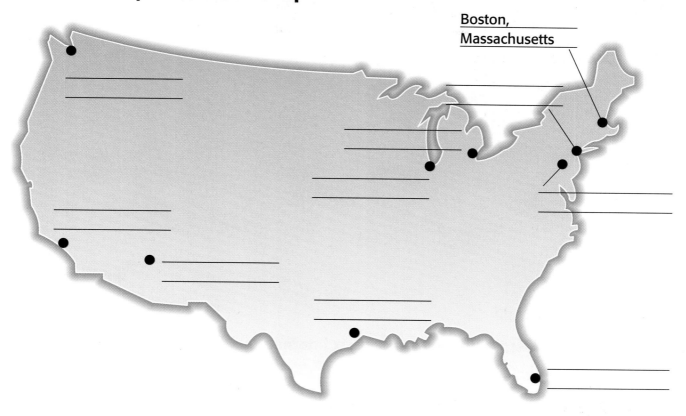

Boston,
_____
Massachusetts

Boston, Massachusetts	Los Angeles, California	New York City, New York
Chicago, Illinois	Miami, Florida	Phoenix, Arizona
Detroit, Michigan	Philadelphia, Pennsylvania	Seattle, Washington
Houston, Texas		

 D. *Or* questions. Ask and answer with a partner.

1. Is Boston small or large?

2. Is Los Angeles hot or cold?

3. Is Miami near the mountains or near the ocean?

4. Is Seattle in the north or in the south?

5. Is New York City clean or dirty?

6. Are the people in Houston friendly or unfriendly?

7. Are the stores in Chicago cheap or expensive?

8. Are the streets in Seattle busy or quiet?

E. Pair practice. Ask and answer questions about your city.

Is your city quiet?

Yes, it is.

Yes, it is.
No, it isn't.

near the ocean

noisy

cheap

crowded

clean

beautiful

quiet

F. As a class, write the names of six international cities. Complete the chart.

City	Nationality	Language
Paris	French	French
1.		
2.		
3.		
4.		
5.		
6.		

G. Complete from the chart.

1. _____ is from _____.
    male classmate   city

2. He is _____, and he speaks _____.
            nationality   language

3. _____ is from _____.
    female classmate   city

4. She is _____, and she speaks _____.
            nationality   language

What city do you want to visit?

**A. Listen and complete.**

Janet   Steven   Caroline and Susan

1. Janet wants to visit _____ because it is _____.

2. Steven wants to visit _____ because it is _____.

3. Caroline and Susan want to visit _____ because it is

   _____.

B. Pair practice. Talk about a city you want to visit.

What city do you want to visit?

I want to visit New York.

Why?

I want to go to New York because it is exciting.

Chicago	Houston	Miami	quiet
Los Angeles	New York	San Francisco	safe
Phoenix	Boston	_____	clean

quiet
safe
clean
interesting
beautiful
cheap
hot
friendly
exciting
fun

City Populations

 A. Listen.

1.	Miami, Florida	369,253	6.	San Antonio, Texas	1,147,213
2.	Atlanta, Georgia	401,766	7.	Philadelphia, Pennsylvania	1,417,601
3.	Las Vegas, Nevada	418,658	8.	Houston, Texas	1,845,967
4.	Washington, D.C.	519,000	9.	Los Angeles, California	3,633,591
5.	Detroit, Michigan	965,084	10.	New York, New York	7,428,162

 B. Listen and write the populations.

1. Seattle, Washington   563,374

2. Phoenix, Arizona   _____

3. San Francisco, California   _____

4. Boston, Massachusetts   _____

5. Chicago, Illinois   _____

6. Fresno, California   _____

7. Honolulu, Hawaii   _____

8. Dallas, Texas   _____

C. Pronunciation. Practice these numbers with a partner.

1. 2,890,000   (Ankara, Turkey)

2. 34,800,000   (Tokyo, Japan)

3. 17,900,000   (São Paolo, Brazil)

4. 14,350,000   (Cairo, Egypt)

5. 10,150,000   (Paris, France)

6. 1,719,000   (Cali, Colombia)

7. 13,200,000   (Moscow, Russia)

8. 11,800,000   (Shanghai, China)

> The population of Ankara, Turkey, is 2,890,000.

 Which city is this?

A. Look at the photographs. Guess the city.

San Antonio, Texas
Fairbanks, Alaska
San Francisco, California
Chicago, Illinois
New York, New York
Miami, Florida
Honolulu, Hawaii

B. Answer.

1. What state is the city in?
2. Is the city beautiful?
3. Is the city near the mountains or near the ocean?
4. Is the city safe?
5. Is the city exciting?
6. What do you know about the city?

Working Together

Yes, it is.
No, it isn't.

Yes, they are,
No, they aren't.

A. Interview. In a group of three students, ask these questions and complete the chart.

Question	Student 1	Student 2
1. What city are you from?		
2. Is your city in the East, West, North, or South?		
3. Is your city the capital city of your country?		
4. Is your city beautiful?		
5. Is your city busy?		
6. Are the people hardworking?		

B. Complete.

1. _____ is from _____.
   Student 1   city

2. _____ is _____.
   city   location

3. _____ **is / isn't** the capital city.

4. _____ **is / isn't** _____.
                      adjective

5. The people **are / aren't** _____.

6. _____ is from _____.
   Student 2   city

7. _____ is _____.
   city   location

8. _____ **is / isn't** the capital city.

9. _____ **is / isn't** _____.
                      adjective

10. The people **are / aren't** _____.

C. Complete the sentences about the city where you are studying.

Our City

1. Our school is in _____, _____.
   <small>city</small>   <small>state</small>

2. The population of _____ is about _____.
                 <small>city</small>   <small>population</small>

3. The largest city in our state is _____.

4. _____ _____ the capital city.
       <small>city</small>   <small>is / isn't</small>

5. _____ is _____.
       <small>city</small>   <small>adjective</small>

6. _____ is _____.
                     <small>adjective</small>

7. _____ isn't _____

8. _____ isn't _____.

9. The people _____ friendly.
              <small>are / aren't</small>

10. The people _____ hardworking.
               <small>are / aren't</small>

D. Look at the map on the inside back cover of the book. Draw a simple map of your state. Show your city and the capital of your state.

The Big Picture: Chicago, Illinois

A. Can you identify these places and people?

The Brookfield Zoo	The Sears Tower	Blues club
The Art Institute of Chicago	Oprah Winfrey	Wrigley Field
Lake Michigan		

B. Listen.

C. Match.

1. _____ paintings
2. _____ musicians
3. _____ Oprah Winfrey
4. _____ baseball
5. _____ animals
6. _____ office building

a. blues clubs
b. Wrigley Field
c. Art Institute of Chicago
d. Brookfield Zoo
e. Sears Tower
f. TV talk show host

D. Listen again and circle.

Yes   No   **1.** Chicago is in the south of the United States.

Yes   No   **2.** Chicago is near water.

Yes   No   **3.** Spring is a good time to visit Chicago.

Yes   No   **4.** Chicago's summers are hot.

Yes   No   **5.** You can enjoy art and music in Chicago.

Yes   No   **6.** Chicago has one professional sports team.

Yes   No   **7.** Oprah Winfrey is a popular blues musician.

E. *Or* Questions. Ask and answer with a partner.

> Is Chicago a city or a state?
> It's a city.

1. Is Chicago in the midwest or in the south?

2. Are the winters in Chicago warm or cold?

3. Is Chicago near a lake or an ocean?

4. Is Chicago famous for rock music or blues music?

5. Is Wrigley Field for baseball or for football?

6. Is the Brookfield Zoo interesting or boring for children?

7. Is the Sears Tower a large or a small building?

8. Is downtown Chicago quiet or busy?

F. Complete with *is, isn't, are,* or *aren't*.

1. It _____is_____ fun for people to see professional sports in Chicago.

2. Lake Michigan _____ a beautiful lake.

3. Winters in Chicago _____ hot and humid.

4. Downtown Chicago _____ busy.

5. The Sears Tower _____ a small building.

6. The Art Institute of Chicago _____ a boring museum.

7. The Brookfield Zoo _____ fun for children.

8. Chicago blues clubs _____ exciting and interesting.

Reading: Seattle, Washington

A. Before You Read.

1. Where is Washington state?

2. Is Seattle in the north or the south of the state?

3. Is Seattle near the mountains? Is it near the ocean?

Seattle is the largest city in Washington state. The population of Seattle is 563,374. It is in the northwest of the United States. It is in a beautiful location near the Pacific Ocean and Canada. Seattle is one of the major seaports in the United States. You can find many boats and houseboats in the water near Seattle. When the weather is clear, you can see the famous sleeping volcano, Mount Rainier.

Seattle is a beautiful city, but it is a rainy city. It gets 36.2 inches, or 92 cm, of rain every year.

Many people know Seattle because of the Space Needle. You can take an elevator to the top of the Space Needle. On the top floor, there is a restaurant that revolves 360°. You can see all of Seattle.

There are many large companies in Seattle. One develops computer software. Another makes coffee. A third sells books on-line.

The University of Washington is in Seattle, and there are many professional sports teams in Seattle. You can see that Seattle is a good place for a vacation, for work, and for relaxation.

B. Circle the answer.

Yes	No	1.	Seattle is a large city.
Yes	No	2.	Seattle is in the Southwest of the United States.
Yes	No	3.	Seattle has warm, sunny weather all year.
Yes	No	4.	Many large companies are in Seattle.
Yes	No	5.	Seattle is a good place for a vacation.

C. Which adjectives describe Seattle?

Writing Our Stories: My City

A. Read.

My name is Steven Lee. I am from Taipei, Taiwan. Taipei is the largest city in Taiwan. The population of my city is about 7,700,000. Taipei is in the north of the island. It has mountains and rivers. My city is big, and it is interesting. The Taipei City Zoo is a famous zoo. The National Palace Museum has a wonderful collection of Chinese art. The weather in Taipei is good all year, but it is often humid. The Taiwanese people are hardworking and friendly.

B. Write.

I am from _____, _____. The
                       city   country

population of my city is about _____. It is _____.
                               population   location

My city is _____. _____ is _____.
           large / small   city   adjective

_____ is _____ and _____.

The people in my city are _____ and

_____

_____

_____

_____

Writing Note
Use a comma between the name of a city and the name of a country: Taipei, Taiwan.

Practicing on Your Own

A. Answer.

1. Is your city near the mountains?   _____

2. Is your city safe at night?   _____

3. Are the people in your city friendly?   _____

4. Are the streets in your city clean?   _____

5. Is your city expensive to live in?   _____

6. Is your city fun?   _____

7. Is your city exciting?   _____

8. Are the buildings in your city large?   _____

B. Complete the sentences with an adjective.

1. I want to visit Chicago because it's _____.

2. I want to visit Seattle because it's _____.

3. I want to visit Miami because it's _____.

4. I want to visit Phoenix because it's _____.

5. I want to visit _____ because _____.

6. I want to visit _____ because _____.

C. Complete about the city where you live now.

is   isn't   are   aren't

1. My city _____ big.

2. The streets _____ clean.

3. The summers _____ hot.

4. The people _____ hardworking.

5. The people _____ friendly.

6. The stores _____ expensive.

7. My city _____ near an ocean.

8. My city _____ interesting.

Learning Tip

We come to class a few minutes early.
We give each other spelling tests.

- ☐ I like this idea.
- ☐ I don't like this idea.
- ☐ I'm going to try this idea.

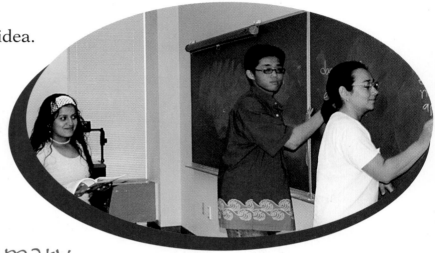

Grammar Summary

▶ **1. Want / Wants**

I **want** to go to New York City because it's exciting.

We **want** to go to Chicago because it's a good sports town.

He **wants** to go to Miami because it's hot and sunny.

She **wants** to go to Denver because it's a good place for winter sports.

▶ **2. Yes / No questions**

Is Chicago in the Midwest?	Yes, it **is.**
Is Seattle in the Midwest?	No, it **isn't.**
Are winters cold in Chicago?	Yes, they **are.**
Are summers hot in Seattle?	No, they **aren't.**

▶ **3. Or questions**

Is Chicago in the north **or** in the south?	It's in the north.
Are the streets in Chicago quiet **or** busy?	They're busy.

7 Downtown

A. Listen and repeat.

Stores

bank

bakery

bookstore

coffee shop

laundromat

shoe store

supermarket

drugstore

Places Downtown

City Hall

library

police station

park

post office

hospital

parking lot

Prepositions

The bank is **on the corner of** First Street and Main Street.

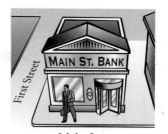

Mr. Garcia is standing **in front of** the bank.

Mr. Garcia is standing **behind** the bank.

Mr. Garcia is standing **next to** the bank.

Mr. Garcia is standing **across from** the bank.

Mr. Garcia is standing **between** the bank and the coffee shop.

B. Complete.

1. I can mail a letter at the _____ post office _____.

2. I can borrow books at the _____.

3. I can buy food at the _____.

4. I can buy a book at the _____.

5. I can wash my clothes at the _____.

6. I can deposit money at the _____.

7. I can get a prescription filled at the _____.

8. I can walk in the _____.

9. I can buy sneakers at the _____.

Active Grammar: Prepositions

 A. Listen and complete the map.

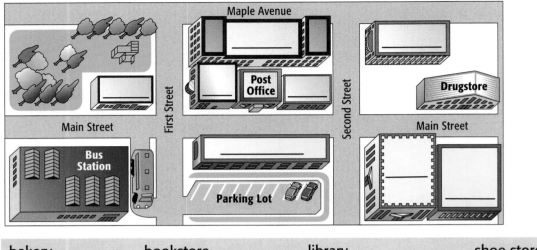

bakery	bookstore	library	shoe store
bank	coffee shop	laundromat	supermarket

B. Pair practice. Talk about the locations on the map above.

Where's the _____?

It's on _____.

C. Complete. Look at the map above.

across from	between	on
behind	next to	on the corner of

1. The supermarket is _____across from_____ the bank.

2. The parking lot is _____ the supermarket.

3. The bank is _____ First Street and Main Street.

4. The post office is _____ the bank and the coffee shop.

5. The bakery is _____ the park.

6. The laundromat is _____ Second Street.

7. The bus station is _____ the parking lot.

8. The bookstore is _____ Main Street and Second Street.

Reading a Map

A. Talk about the map.

The bookstore is next to the bakery.
The parking lot is behind the school.

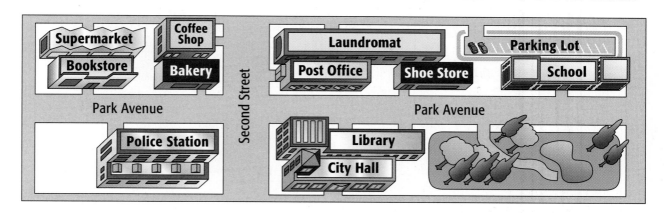

Supermarket
Bookstore
Coffee Shop
Bakery
Park Avenue
Second Street
Laundromat
Post Office
Shoe Store
Parking Lot
School
Park Avenue
Police Station
Library
City Hall

B. Write the locations of five buildings.

1. _____

2. _____

3. _____

4. _____

5. _____

C. Pronunciation. Listen and repeat the conversations.

1. **A:** Where's the shoe store?

   B: It's on Park Avenue.

   A: On Park Avenue?

   B: Yes.

2. **A:** Where's the parking lot?

   B: It's behind the school.

   A: Behind the school?

   B: Yes.

3. **A:** Where's the park?

   B: It's next to the library.

   A: Next to the library?

   B: Yes.

4. **A:** Where's the bakery?

   B: It's across from the police station.

   A: Across from the police station?

   B: Yes.

 Practice these conversations with a partner.

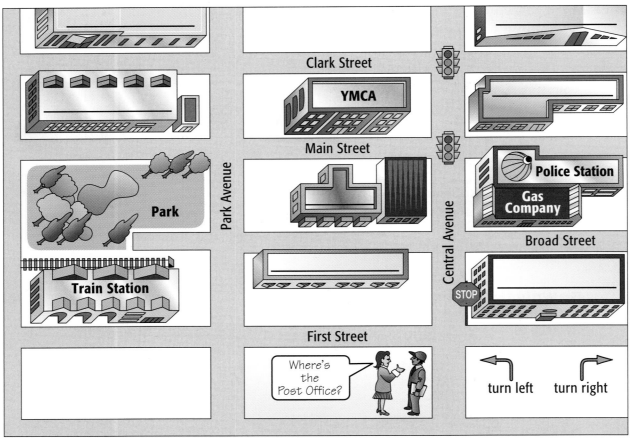

A. Read and write these locations on the map.

1. **A:** Where's the post office?

   B: Walk two blocks to Broad Street.

   Turn left.

   The post office is on your left.

traffic light

2. **A:** Where's the art museum?

   B: Walk four blocks to the second traffic light. That's Clark Street.

   Turn left.

   The art museum is about two blocks up on your right.

3. **A:** Where's the high school?

   B: Walk one block to the first stop sign. That's First Street.

   Turn right.

   The high school is on your left.

stop sign

B. Listen and write the locations on the map.

    1. City Hall   **2.** library   **3.** hospital   **4.** aquarium

C. Read and complete.

traffic light	stop sign	right	left
Clark	Main	Broad	First

    1. A: Where's the gas company?

       B: Walk two blocks to _____Broad_____ Street.

       Turn _____.

       The gas company is on your _____.

    2. A: Where's the train station?

       B: Walk one block to the first _____.

       That's _____ Street.

       Turn _____.

       The train station is two blocks up on your _____.

    3. A: Where's the park?

       B: Walk two blocks to _____ Street.

       Turn _____.

       The park is about two blocks up, in front of you.

D. Write the directions to each of these locations.

    1. City Hall   **2.** the police station   **3.** the aquarium

Walk _____ blocks.
Walk _____ blocks to the first _____.
That's _____ Street.
Turn right.
Turn left.
The _____ is on your right/left.

☀ The Public Library

A. Ask and answer questions about the library.

> Where are the children's books?

> They're downstairs.

1. the reference books
2. the new books
3. the maps

4. the periodicals
5. the computers
6. the newspapers

B. Complete these sentences about your local library.

1. The library is on _____.

2. The telephone number of the library is _____.

3. I **have / don't have** a library card.

Working Together

A. Write the name of a store or location in your community.

1. park: <u>Central Park</u>
2. hospital: _____
3. supermarket: _____
4. drugstore: _____
5. bakery: _____
6. drugstore: _____
7. bank: _____
8. bookstore: _____
9. music store: _____
10. movie theater: _____
11. shoe store: _____

B. Give directions.

The hospital in this area is _____.

It is on _____.
street

For an emergency, I need to call _____.
telephone number

Write directions from your school to the hospital.

_____

_____

_____

_____

_____

A. Listen.

B. Listen and circle.

1. **a.** Elena is.
   b. Jane is.
   c. Mrs. Lee is.

2. **a.** Michael is.
   b. Luisa is.
   c. Michael and Luisa are.

3. **a.** Officer Ortiz is.
   b. Mr. Thomas is.
   c. Mark is.

4. **a.** Officer Ortiz is.
   b. Jane is.
   c. Mrs. Lee is.

5. **a.** Mark is.
   b. Joseph is.
   c. Jane is.

6. **a.** Joseph is.
   b. Jane is.
   c. Luisa is.

7. **a.** Joseph is.
   b. Officer Ortiz is.
   c. Michael and Luisa are.

8. **a.** Mr. Thomas is.
   b. Mrs. Lee is.
   c. Officer Ortiz is.

C. Circle and complete.

1. The playground is _____on_____ Smith Street.
   a. across from   (b.) on   c. between

2. City Hall is _____ the playground.
   a. across from   b. next to   c. on the corner of

3. The coffee shop is _____ the bakery.
   a. next to   b. between   c. behind

4. The parking lot is _____ the laundromat.
   a. across from   b. behind   c. between

5. Jane and Joseph are sitting _____ the coffee shop.
   a. behind   b. in front of   c. next to

6. The police station is _____ City Hall.
   a. across from   b. behind   c. on

7. Officer Ortiz is standing _____ Mrs. Lee's car.
   a. next to   b. on   c. in front of

D. Complete with the name of a person(s) in the picture.

1. _____Officer Ortiz_____ is behind the bookstore.

2. _____ is between the bookstore and the bank.

3. _____ are in front of the coffee shop.

4. _____ are in front of City Hall.

5. _____ is on the corner of North Main Street and Smith Street.

E. Complete.

1. Mr. Thomas _____is talking_____ to the other driver.

2. Elena _____ the children.

3. The children _____.

4. Joseph and Jane _____ at tables.

5. Joseph _____ a newspaper.

6. Mark _____ at the coffee shop.

7. Michael and Luisa _____ married.

watch
read
sit
✓talk
work
play
get

Every Saturday morning, my son and I go to the public library. The library is only four blocks from our apartment. We can walk there.

My son and I have library cards. We go to the children's section, and he takes out books and videos about animals. He can borrow books for one month, but he can only borrow a video for three days.

Story Time is at 10:00. He stays downstairs and listens to the librarian read stories. I go upstairs and take a computer class. I don't have a computer at home. I am learning how to use the Internet and how to send e-mail to my family. At the library, I can use the computer for free. After my class, I stop in the reference section and read a newspaper from my country for a few minutes.

The library is a wonderful place for both me and my son. And best of all, it's free!

A. What can you do at the library?

- ☐ **1.** I can borrow books.
- ☐ **2.** I can borrow videos.
- ☐ **3.** I can do my homework in the library.
- ☐ **4.** I can buy magazines.
- ☐ **5.** I can use the Internet.
- ☐ **6.** I can read books to my children.
- ☐ **7.** I can read the newspaper.
- ☐ **8.** I can leave my child for the day.
- ☐ **9.** I can get a library card.

Writing Our Stories:
Our School

A. Read.

I am a student at Union County College in Elizabeth, New Jersey. Our school is on West Jersey Street. West Jersey Street is a busy street. The traffic is heavy and noisy all day. There are many stores and buildings on West Jersey Street. Our school is between a small parking lot and the gas company. There is a large clothing store across the street. Our school is convenient to transportation. The train station is across the street, and the bus stop is on the corner. We have one problem. Because our school is in a city, it is difficult to find a parking space.

B. Write about the location of your school.

I am a student at _____ in _____,
                                 school   town

_____. Our school in on _____.
             state   street

The traffic is _____ and _____.

Our school is _____

_____

_____

_____

_____

_____

Writing Note
Read your story two or three times. Check the spelling.

A. Look at the map. Complete the sentences.

1. Where _____ the bank?

   It's _____ the bakery.

2. Where _____ the school?

   It's _____ the park.

3. Where _____ the children?

   They _____ in the _____.

4. What _____ doing?

   They _____.

5. Where _____?

   _____.

6. Where _____?

   _____.

7. Where _____?

   _____.

8. Where _____?

   _____.

Looking at Forms: Library Card Application

A. Complete.

Public Library Card Application

_____	_____	_____	___/___/___
Last name	First name	MI	Today's date

☐ Adult ☐ Child   ____ - ____ - ____   _____
 Social Security Number   (If child, signature of parent/guardian)

_____
Address

_____   _____   _____
City   State   Zip Code

Telephone: (____) _____ - _____

Grammar Summary

> ▶ **1. Prepositions**
>
> Where is the library?   It's **on** Maple Avenue.
>
> Where are the foreign newspapers?   They are **next to** the computers.

> ▶ **2. *Who* questions**
>
> **Who** is watching the children?   Elena is.
>
> **Who** is drinking coffee?   Joseph and Jane are.

> ▶ **3. *Can* statements**
>
> I **can** mail a letter at the post office.

Money

Dictionary: Coins and Bills

 A. Listen and repeat.

Coins

a penny	a nickel	a dime	a quarter
one cent	five cents	ten cents	twenty-five cents
$.01	$.05	$.10	$.25

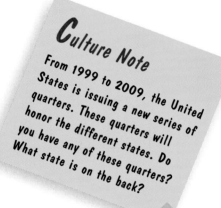

Culture Note

From 1999 to 2009, the United States is issuing a new series of quarters. These quarters will honor the different states. Do you have any of these quarters? What state is on the back?

Bills

a dollar
$1.00

five dollars
$5.00

ten dollars
$10.00

twenty dollars
$20.00

Active Grammar: *How much Questions*

A. Listen and repeat.

a.	4¢	$.04		f.	50¢	$.50
b.	10¢	$.10		g.	62¢	$.62
c.	25¢	$.25		h.	75¢	$.75
d.	30¢	$.30		i.	85¢	$.85
e.	35¢	$.35		j.	99¢	$.99

> **Money**
> There are three ways to write cents.
> ten cents
> 10¢
> $.10

B. Write the amount.

a.

_____

b.

_____

c.

_____

d.

_____

e.

_____

> Sit in a group.
> Take out your change
> Count it together.
> Write the amount.
> Who has the most change?

C. Listen and write the amount.

a. ____$.02____   d. _____   g. _____

b. _____   e. _____   h. _____

c. _____   f. _____   i. _____

 Bills

> **Dollars and Cents**
> $ 2.50: two <u>dollars</u> and fifty <u>cents</u>   *or*   two fifty
> $ 10.99: ten <u>dollars</u> and ninety-nine <u>cents</u>   *or*   ten ninety-nine.
> $498.79: four hundred and ninety-eight dollars and seventy-nine cents
>   *or*   four ninety-eight seventy-nine.

 A. Listen and repeat.

a. $1.00	**d.** $4.99	**g.** $127.98
b. $1.50	**e.** $17.49	**h.** $249.99
c. $2.75	**f.** $59.50	**i.** $629.77

 B. Listen and write the amount.

a. _____$1.00_____   **f.** _____

b. _____   **g.** _____

c. _____   **h.** _____

d. _____   **i.** _____

e. _____

> ***Culture Note***
> The dollar is the monetary unit of the United States. What is the monetary unit in your country?

 C. Listen and repeat.

13	14	15	16	17	18	19	20
30	40	50	60	70	80	90	100

(Circle.)

a. 13 30		**h.** $13.50 $13.15
b. 14 40		**i.** $15.99 $50.99
c. 15 50		**j.** $19.99 $90.99
d. 16 60		**k.** $14.40 $14.14
e. 17 70		**l.** $17.20 $70.20
f. 18 80		**m.** $16.16 $60.16
g. 19 90		**n.** $18.75 $80.75

Looking at Forms: Checks

A. Read.

	Date 3/9/02
Pay to the order of _Central Camera_	$ 167.12
one hundred sixty-seven and $^{12}/_{00}$	DOLLARS
First National Bank	_Juan Hernandez_

B. Write these check amounts.

$21.40   twenty-one and $^{40}/_{00}$

$137.95   one hundred thirty-seven and $^{95}/_{00}$

$359.80   three hundred fifty-nine and $^{80}/_{00}$

a. $7.50 _____

b. $34.25 _____

c. $59.49 _____

d. $137.12 _____

e. $429.67 _____

W_riting Note_

Put the cents amount over /00.

C. Complete these checks.

To: The Electronics Center	Date _____
	Pay to the order of _____ $ _____
$84.95	_____ DOLLARS
	First National Bank _____

To: United Credit	Date _____
	Pay to the order of _____ $ _____
$237.52	_____ DOLLARS
	First National Bank _____

☀ I need a fax machine.

A. Write seven other items you can buy in an electronics store.

fax machine
answering machine
TV
speakers
computer

_____

_____

_____

_____

_____

_____

_____

 B. Pronunciation. Listen. How many syllables do you hear?

store	1	notebook	2
sale	1	stereo	3
printer	2	camcorder	3
computer	3	tapes	1
telephone	3	headphones	2
CDs	2	VCR	3
batteries	3	speakers	2
scanner	2	camera	3
movies	2	stereo	3
disk	1	games	1

C. Look at the list in Exercise B. Write five singular words. Write five plural words.

Singular	Plural
_____	_____
_____	_____
_____	_____
_____	_____
_____	_____

D. Label the computer with a partner.

CD-ROM	keyboard	mouse
floppy disk	keys	mouse pad
monitor	speakers	screen

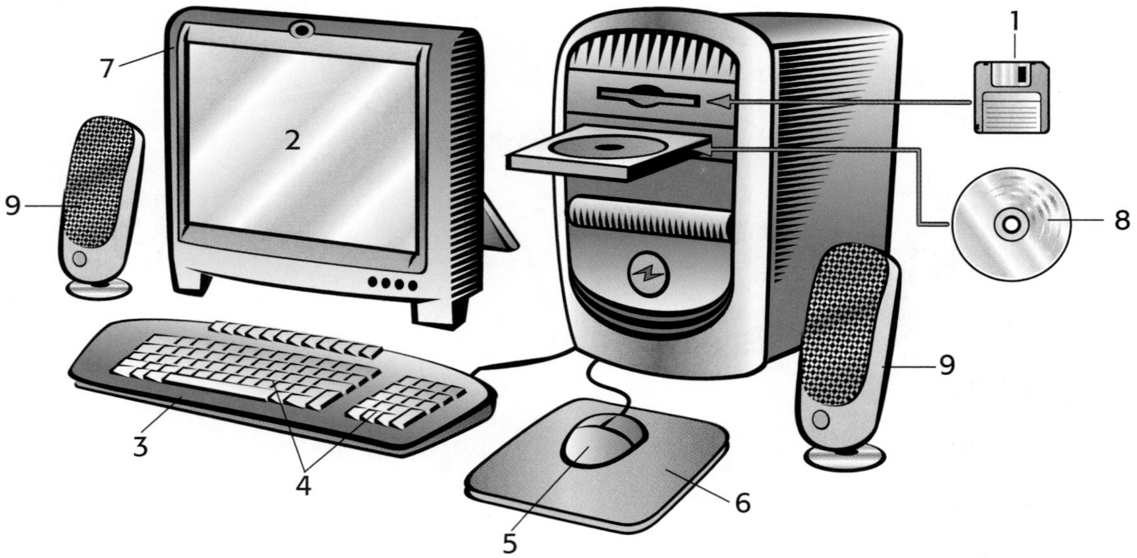

1. _____   5. _____

2. _____   6. _____

3. _____   7. _____

4. _____   8. _____

9. _____

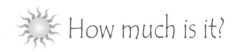 How much is it?

A. Pair practice.

A: How much is this camera?

B: It's on sale. It's $179.

A: I'll take it.

$349
27" TV

$179
VCR

$139
Speaker phone

$219
Printer

$299
Stereo system

$199
Scanner

$179
Camera

How much are they?

A. Pair practice.

A: How much are these headphones?

B: They're on sale. They're $29.95.

A: I'll take them.

Working Together

A. Sit in a group of four students. Talk about the places you like to shop.

1. I shop at _____ for clothes.

2. I shop at _____ for shoes.

3. I shop at _____ for food.

4. I shop at _____ for sports equipment.

5. I shop at _____ for CDs.

6. I shop at _____ for toys.

7. I shop at _____ for _____.

B. Sit in a group. Complete with a price.

1. A first-class stamp is _____.

2. A local telephone call is _____.

3. The local newspaper is _____.

4. A gallon of regular gas is _____.

5. A cup of coffee is _____.

6. A CD is _____.

7. A video rental is _____.

8. A movie at the movie theater is _____.

9. A round-trip airline ticket to my country is _____.

10. A computer is _____.

C. Bring in sales circulars from different stores. Sit in a group and discuss.

Where is the sale? Do you shop there?

What kind of store is it? When is the sale?

List four items on sale. What is the regular price? What is the sale price?

D. Complete about a bank in your area.

Bank: _____

Street: _____

The bank is open from _____ to _____ on weekdays.

The bank is open late on _____ night.

The bank is open on Saturday from _____ to _____.

 E. Interview a partner. Check your partner's answers.

ATM: Automated Teller Machine

How do you pay for . . .	I pay cash.	I use a credit card.	I write a check.	I get a money order.	I use my ATM card.
gas					
rent					
food					
your telephone bill					
your electric bill					
clothes					

F. Put these ATM steps in order.

_____ Select *Withdraw cash*.

_____ Take your cash.

___1___ Insert your ATM card.

_____ Take your receipt.

___2___ Put in your PIN number.

_____ Remember your ATM card!

_____ Choose the amount you want.

A. Circle the equipment you see in the store.

TVs	camcorders	speakers
headphones	electronic dictionaries	scanners
game systems	computers	fax machines
DVDs	printers	telephones

 B. Listen.

C. Listen again and write the correct name under each person.

Marta	George	Mr. and Mrs. Jackson
Tammy and Sean	Tamara	

D. Complete.

1. Marta _____*is standing*_____ in front of the TVs.

2. Tammy and Sean _____ a baby.

   They _____ at camcorders.

3. George _____ at DVDs.

4. Tamara _____ English.

   She _____ an electronic dictionary.

5. Mr. and Mrs. Jackson _____
   at the store with their grandson.

   He _____ them buy a computer.

> is studying
> is looking
> is buying
> are
> ✓ is standing
> are looking
> is helping
> are expecting

E. Listen to each conversation. Write the item and the price.

Conversation 1: _____*Russian-English dictionary*_____ $ ___*$39.99*___

Conversation 2: _____ $ _____

Conversation 3: _____ $ _____

Conversation 4: _____ $ _____

F. Match.

1. This is a nice camcorder. Is it easy to use?   It's on sale for $799. And there's a $100 rebate.

2. Can I connect it to my TV?   Yes, it's very easy to use.

3. How long is the warranty?   Yes, you can connect it to your TV or your computer.

4. How much is it?   Send this card and a copy of your receipt to the manufacturer. They will send you $100.

5. What's a rebate?   It's one year.

Reading

A. Before You Read

1. Do you shop at sales?
2. Where can you find information about sales?

July 4th Sale! Electronics City
July 4th and 5th 9 A.M. to 10 P.M.

Notebook ~~$1,699~~ $1,299

36" Stereo TV $749

Cordless Phone with Caller ID and Answering System
Save $20! ONLY $69

NOW ONLY $249
DVD Player

Digital Camera $499
$599-$100
Manufacturer's Mail-in Rebate

SPECIAL $849
STEREO SYSTEM, includes receiver & five speakers

B. Answer.

1. What's the name of this store?
2. When is the sale?
3. How much will you save on the notebook computer?
4. What features does the cordless phone include?
5. What size is the TV?
6. What does the stereo system include?
7. How much is the digital camera?
8. Is this a good sale?

A. Read.

I have a home entertainment center. In my living room, I have a large-screen TV with four speakers. I have a DVD player, too. I'm saving my money now for a video camera. I want to take pictures of my vacation. The camera I want is $795. I want to buy it on sale.

B. Write. What electronic equipment do you have? What are you planning to buy?

I have a(n) _____. I also have a(n) _____.

I want a(n) _____.

I'm saving my money for a _____. _____

_____

_____

_____

Writing Note

Use capital letters for these words: TV, VCR, DVD, PC.

Practicing on Your Own

A. Write the amount.

Dollars and Cents
$ 2.50: two <u>dollars</u> and fifty <u>cents</u>
$10.99: ten <u>dollars</u> and ninety-nine <u>cents</u>

a. $1.00   _____ one dollar _____

b. $4.50   _____

c. $7.98   _____

d. $18.75   _____

e. $79.63   _____

f. $135.72 _____

g. $199.00 _____

B. Complete each question with *is* or *are*. Write the answer.

It's $_____.   They're $_____.

1. How much ____are____ the speakers?   ____They're $89 each.____

2. How much _____ the DVD player?   _____

3. How much _____ batteries?   _____

4. How much _____ the CDs?   _____

5. How much _____ the electronic dictionary? _____

6. How much _____ the scanner?   _____

7. How much _____ the headphones?   _____

Looking at Forms: Mail-In Rebate

A. Complete this rebate form.

Many electronics stores offer mail-in rebates. You must send an application form and your receipt to the manufacturer.

$399
$449 – $50
Manufacturer's
Mail-in Rebate

Name: _____
                Last   First

Address: _____

City: _____ State: _____ Zip code: _____

Phone number: (_____) _____

E-mail address: _____

Product (circle):   printer   fax   scanner   copier   monitor   computer

Model number: _____

Store: _____

Date of purchase: _____

Signature: _____

Send this form and your receipt to the manufacturer.

Grammar Summary

▶ 1. *How much* questions

How much is the printer?	It's $129.00.
How much is it?	It's $129.00.
How much are the speakers?	They're $249.00.
How much are they?	They're $249.00.

▶ 2. Dollars and cents

$4.95: four dollars and ninety-five cents

     four ninety-five

▶ 3. Writing check amounts

$4.95: *four and* 95/00

9 Working at the Mall

Dictionary: Jobs

A. Listen and repeat.

Jobs

hairstylist
A hairstylist cuts hair.

manicurist
A manicurist colors nails.

cashier
A cashier takes money.

security guard
A security guard
watches customers.

cook
A cook prepares food.

waiter
A waiter serves food.

salesperson
A salesperson helps customers.

pharmacist
A pharmacist fills prescriptions.

photographer
A photographer takes pictures.

florist
A florist sells flowers.

painter
A painter paints walls and ceilings.

custodian
A custodian cleans floors.

B. Complete.

1. A hairstylist _____cuts_____ hair.

2. A custodian _____ the floor.

3. A security guard _____ customers.

4. A florist _____ flowers.

5. A cook _____ food.

6. A manicurist _____ nails.

7. A pharmacist _____ prescriptions.

8. A photographer _____ pictures.

cleans
sells
takes
colors
✓cuts
watches
fills
prepares

C. Complete.

1. A _____ stands all day.

2. A _____ sits at work.

3. A _____ has to write orders.

4. A _____ wears a uniform.

5. A _____ talks to customers.

D. Discuss other jobs.

1. Who works at your school?

2. Who works in an office?

3. Who works in a hospital?

4. Who works at a mall?

A. Complete.

1. Luis works at _____ Cosimo's _____. He's a _____ waiter _____.

2. Richard works at _____. He's a _____.

3. Marie works at _____. She's a _____.

4. Sam works at _____. He's a _____.

5. Carlos works at _____. He's a _____.

6. Sheri works at _____. She's a _____.

7. Kenji works at _____. He's a _____.

B. Read.

A: Where does Ahmed work?

B: He works at the Parkside Mall.

A: What does he do?

B: He's a security guard.

> **Present Tense**
> I work at the mall.
> She work<u>s</u> at the mall.
> He work<u>s</u> at the mall.

 C. Pair practice. Talk about the jobs in the mall.

D. Read the schedule. Complete the information below.

	Sunday	Monday	Tuesday	Wednesday	Thursday	Friday	Saturday
Sam			3–11	3–11	3–11	3–11	3–11
Luis		12–5	12–5			12–5	12–5

1. Sam works __8__ hours a day.

2. Sam works _____ days a week.

3. Sam works **full time / part time.**

4. Luis works _____ hours a day.

5. Luis works _____ days a week.

6. Luis works **full time / part time.**

7. I work _____ hours a day.

8. I work _____ days a week.

9. I work **full time / part time.**

> Full time: 35–40 hours a week
> Part time: less than that a week

 **A. Listen and repeat.**

two o'clock
2:00

two oh-five
2:05

two ten
2:10

two fifteen
2:15

two thirty
2:30

two forty
2:40

two forty-five
2:45

two fifty
2:50

two fifty-five
2:55

three o'clock
3:00

B. Show the time on the clocks. Say the time.

1:00

6:30

7:15

11:45

2:10

3:40

5:25

4:55

 C. Listen and show the time on the clocks.

a.
b.
c.
d.

What time do you get up?

A. Complete about your schedule.

I get up at
__:__.

I eat breakfast at
__:__.

I leave the house at
__:__.

I work from
__:__ to __:__.

I eat dinner at
__:__.

I study from
__:__ to __:__.

I get home at
__:__.

I watch TV from
__:__ to __:__.

I go to bed at
__:__.

B. Complete. Use *at* or *from/to*.

1. I get up ___at___ 6:00.

2. I eat breakfast _____ 7:00.

3. I go to school _____ 9:00 _____ 12:00.

4. I eat lunch _____ 1:00.

5. I work _____ 3:00 _____ 11:00.

6. I go to bed _____ 12:00.

> **Prepositions**
> I go to school <u>at</u> 7:20.
> I study <u>from</u> 7:30 <u>to</u> 9:00.

C. Sit with a partner. Ask the questions and complete the times.

	Me	My Partner
1. What time do you get up?		
2. What time do you eat breakfast?		
3. What time do you leave the house?		
4. What time do you work?		
5. What time do you study?		
6. What time do you go to bed?		

D. Complete about the chart.

> **Present Tense**
> I get up at 7:00.
> He get<u>s</u> up at 7:00.

1. My partner gets up <u>at</u> ___:___.

2. My partner eats breakfast _____ ___:___.

3. My partner leaves the house _____ ___:___.

4. My partner works <u>from</u> ___:___ <u>to</u> ___:___.

5. My partner studies _____ ___:___ _____ ___:___.

6. My partner goes to bed _____ ___:___.

 My Job

A. Read.

A: Where do you work?

B: I work at Photo-Mart.

A: What do you do?

B: I'm a photographer. I take pictures of children and families. I take passport photos, too.

A: Do you work full time or part time?

B: I work full time.

A: What's your schedule?

B: I work from Wednesday to Sunday, from 11:00 to 7:00. I have Monday and Tuesday off.

A: Do you like your job?

B: Yes, I do.

B. Listen and complete.

1. Marie works at _____ Family Pharmacy _____.
2. She's a _____.
3. She works **full time / part time**.
4. She works from _____ to _____.
5. She works from ___:___ to ___:___.
6. She **likes / doesn't like** her job.

7. Juan works at _____ The Flower Basket _____.
8. He's a _____.
9. He works **full time / part time**.
10. He works from _____ to _____.
11. He works from ___:___ to ___:___.
12. He **likes / doesn't like** his job.

C. Practice this conversation with a partner.

A: Where do you work?

B: I work at _____.

A: What do you do?

B: I'm a _____.

A: Do you work full time or part time?

B: I work _____.

A: What's your schedule?

B: I work from _____ to _____, from ___:___ to ___:___.

I have _____ and _____ off.

A: Do you like your job?

B: _____

 Sam's Day

 A. Pronunciation. Listen and repeat.

/s/	/z/	/əz/
get—gets	drive—drives	watch—watches
work—works	go—goes	punch—punches
take—takes	study—studies	

Pronounce these words.

1. eats   3. prepares   5. brushes

2. lives   4. sells   6. cuts

 B. Listen and repeat. Link the final *s* with the following vowel.

1. Sam lives_alone.

2. He gets_up at 8:00 in the morning.

3. He takes_a shower.

4. He studies_English from 9:00 to 12:00.

5. He punches_in at 4:00.

6. He works_at Cosimo's five or six days a week.

Practice these sentences with a partner.

 C. Complete the story. Then read the story to your partner.

Sam ___lives___ alone in a small apartment. He is busy all day. He ___gets___ up at 8:00 in the morning. He _____ a shower; then he gets dressed. Sam doesn't eat breakfast. He drives to school and _____ English from 9:00 to 12:00. He goes home and _____ lunch at 1:00. Sam leaves for work at 3:30, and he punches in at 4:00. Sam is a cook at the Parkside Mall. He _____ at Cosimo's five or six days a week. He _____ pizza and Italian food. He _____ from 4:00 to 11:00. He takes two breaks. Sam _____ dinner at the restaurant at 9:00. Sam goes home at 11:30. He _____ TV for an hour; then he _____ to bed at 1:00.

prepares
goes
studies
✓lives
takes
✓gets
works
eats
works
watches
eats

Working Together

A. Laura's Day. Laura has a busy day. She works full time, and she goes to school. Sit with a partner. Put her schedule in order from 1 to 10.

B. Write a story about Laura's day.

Laura gets up at . . .

_____

_____

_____

_____

_____

_____

_____

The Big Picture: The CD Den

employer: owner, company
boss: supervisor, manager
employee: worker

A. Listen.

B. Check (✓) *Yes* or *No*.

		Yes	No
1.	Eric is the manager of the CD Den.	✓	☐
2.	He works part time.	☐	☐
3.	This store sells CDs and tapes.	☐	☐
4.	The store opens at 12:00.	☐	☐
5.	Mei-Lin is the assistant manager.	☐	☐
6.	All the other employees are full time.	☐	☐
7.	Most employees are students.	☐	☐
8.	The store is busy on the weekends.	☐	☐
9.	There is a security guard during the week.	☐	☐
10.	The security guard wears a uniform.	☐	☐

C. Circle the correct verb.

Present Tense
I work at the mall.
She works at the mall.
He works at the mall.

1. I (work) / works full time.
2. Mei-Lin **work** / **works** full time.
3. The store **open** / **opens** at 10:00.
4. The store **have** / **has** two managers.
5. The security guard **walk** / **walks** around the store.
6. Many employees **work** / **works** part time.

D. Listen. Write the day and times.

Sunday	Monday	Tuesday	Wednesday	Thursday	Friday	Saturday

1. James can work on ___Monday___ from _5_ : _00_ to _9_ : _00_ .
2. Gloria can work on _____ from ___:___ to ___:___ .
3. Makiko can work on _____ from ___:___ to ___:___ .
4. Andre can work on _____ from ___:___ to ___:___ .
5. Lucy can work on _____ from ___:___ to ___:___ .

Looking at Forms: A Job Application

A. You are applying for a job at the CD Den. Complete this application.

THE CD DEN

Name: _____
First   Last   Middle Initial

Address: _____
Street

_____
City   State   Zip Code

Telephone Number: (_____)_____

Social Security Number: _____

I can work _____ hours a week.

I can work (circle): Sunday Monday Tuesday Wednesday Thursday Friday Saturday

I can work from ____ : ____ to ____ : ____ .

Reading: Working at the Mall

A. Before You Read. Do you know anyone who works at a mall? What do they do?

Richard is a hairstylist. He works from Tuesday to Saturday. He works 40 hours a week, from 10:00 to 6:00. He is very busy on Friday and Saturday because everyone wants to look good for the weekend. Most of Richard's customers are his "regulars"; they come in once a week for a wash and a blow-dry. Richard enjoys talking with them. Richard stands all day, and he's tired at the end of the day. He takes a long, hot bath when he gets home.

Andre is a cashier at the CD Den. He's a college student, and he goes to school every day. He works two evenings a week and all day Saturday and Sunday. People buy CDs and tapes, and Andre takes their money. Some people pay with cash; other people use credit cards. Andre gives them change and their receipts. Andre likes his job. He can listen to music all day.

B. Check (✓).

	Richard	Andre
1. He works full time.	✓	☐
2. He works part time.	☐	☐
3. He works in the evening.	☐	☐
4. He works all weekend.	☐	☐
5. He goes to school.	☐	☐
6. He stands all day.	☐	☐
7. He has regular customers.	☐	☐

Writing Our Stories:
My Job

A. Read

I am a security guard. I work at the Summit Mall in Westbrook. I work full time. I work 40 hours a week, from Tuesday to Saturday. My hours are from 10:00 to 6:00. I walk up and down the mall all day. I answer questions and give directions. I carry a cell phone. In an emergency, I call the police or the ambulance.

B. Write about your job.

I am a _____ . I work at _____ .
             job   company

It's in _____ , on _____ .
       city   street

I work _____ . I work _____ hours a week.
       full time / part time

_____

_____

_____

_____

Writing Note

The days of the week begin with capital letters: Monday, Tuesday, Wednesday, Thursday, Friday, Saturday, Sunday

The names of companies begin with capital letters: Clothes Closet, Hair Plus, MacDougal's

 Practicing on Your Own

A. What time is it?

It's _____.   It's _____.   It's _____.   It's _____.

B. Write the answer.

No, she works part time.   ✓ She's a manicurist.
She works four days a week.   She works from 10:00 to 6:00.
Yes, she does.   She works at Hair Plus.
She was a hairstylist.

1. What does Sheri do?   _____ She's a manicurist. _____

2. Where does she work?   _____

3. How many days does she work?   _____

4. Does she work full time?   _____

5. What hours does she work?   _____

6. Does she like her job?   _____

7. What was her job in her country?   _____

C. Complete with *at* or *from . . . to.*

at 10:00
from 10:00 to 6:00

Eric gets up ____at____ 8:00. He takes a shower and has a small
breakfast, and then he drives to work. Eric arrives at work _____
9:45. He works _____ 10:00 _____ 6:00 six days a week.
Two nights a week, Eric goes to school _____ 7:00 _____
10:00. He's studying for a degree in business. He studies or watches TV
_____ 10:00 _____ 12:00. He goes to bed _____ 12:30.

Learning Tip

It's important to continue reading in my native language.
I read the newspaper in my language every day.

☐ I like this idea.
☐ I don't like this idea.
☐ I'm going to do this.

Grammar Summary

▶ **1. Present tense**

I work at Hair Plus.

He work**s** at Hair Plus.

She work**s** at Hair Plus.

▶ **2. *Yes/No* questions**

Does he work at Hair Plus?	Yes, he **does.**	No, he **doesn't.**
Do you work at Hair Plus?	Yes, I **do.**	No, I **don't.**

▶ **3. *Wh-* questions**

Where does he work?	He works at Cosimo's.
What does he do?	He's a waiter.
What does he do there?	He takes people's orders.
What hours does he work?	He works from 5:00 to 10:00.

▶ **4. Prepositions: *at, from . . . to***

She gets up **at** 7:00.

She goes to school **from** 8:00 **to** 3:00.

Clothing and Weather

Dictionary: Clothing and Colors

 A. Listen and repeat.

Clothing

shirt

pants

jeans

shorts

jacket

belt

suit

sweater

dress

skirt

blouse

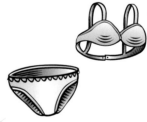

underpants   bra

tie

briefs

T-shirt

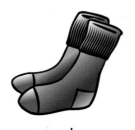

socks

bathing suit

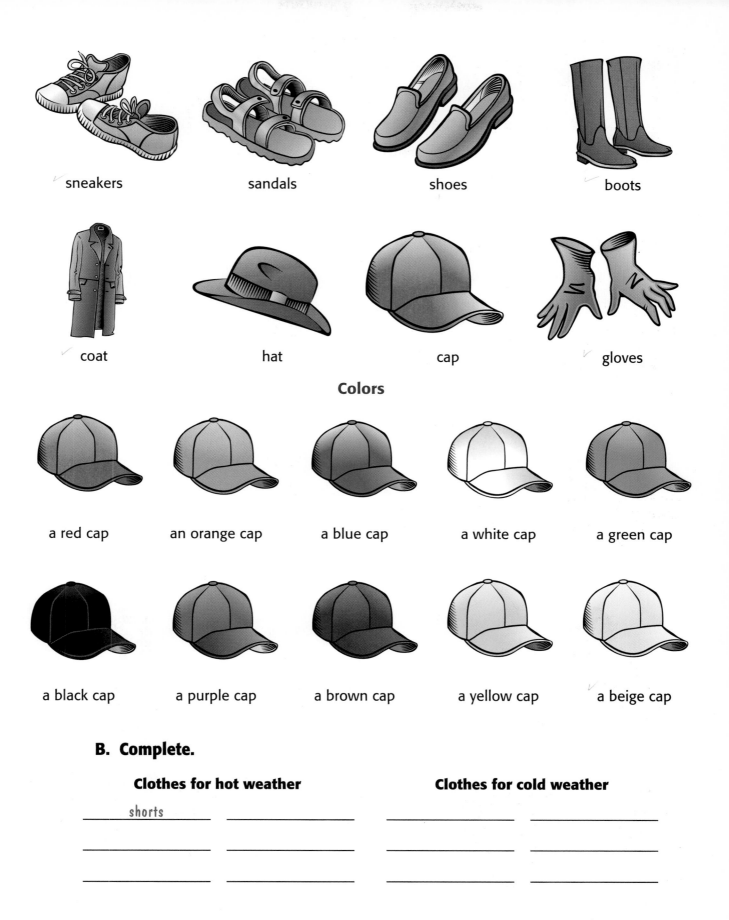

sneakers

sandals

shoes

boots

coat

hat

cap

gloves

Colors

a red cap

an orange cap

a blue cap

a white cap

a green cap

a black cap

a purple cap

a brown cap

a yellow cap

a beige cap

B. Complete.

Clothes for hot weather		**Clothes for cold weather**	
shorts	_____	_____	_____
_____	_____	_____	_____
_____	_____	_____	_____

Active Grammar: Present Continuous

A. Cross out the word that doesn't belong.

1. pants, jeans, shorts, ~~T-shirt~~
2. shirt, blouse, T-shirt, sandals
3. sneakers, sandals, hat, shoes
4. coat, hat, gloves, bathing suit
5. blouse, tie, skirt, dress
6. sweater, briefs, underpants, bra
7. jacket, sweater, coat, shorts

B. Look around your classroom. Who is wearing _____?

> Marek is.
> No one is.

1. Who is wearing sneakers?
2. Who is wearing a sweater?
3. Who is wearing a dress?
4. Who is wearing a white shirt?
5. Who is wearing a tie?
6. Who is wearing sandals?
7. Who is wearing black pants?

C. Discuss with a partner.

> What is Amy wearing?

> She's wearing black pants.

A

B

C

D. Listen. What is Amy wearing? Write the letter of the correct picture.

1. __B__
2. _____
3. _____
4. _____

5. _____
6. _____
7. _____
8. _____

E. Pronunciation. Listen for the stress.

1. Is Amy wearing white pants? No, she's wearing black pants.
2. Is Amy wearing a blue jacket? No, she's wearing a green jacket.
3. Is Amy wearing a red dress? No, she's wearing a blue dress.

Mark the stress.

4. Is Amy wearing a blue belt? No, she's wearing a white belt.
5. Is Amy wearing brown sandals? No, she's wearing white sandals.
6. Is Amy wearing black shorts? No, she's wearing beige shorts.
7. Is Amy wearing a purple shirt? No, she's wearing a green shirt.
8. Is Amy wearing beige socks? No, she's wearing white socks.

Practice these sentences with a partner.

F. Look at the pictures of Amy on page 138. Complete with *a, an,* or *X*.

1. Amy is going to work. She is wearing __X__ black pants and __a__ white blouse. She's wearing _____ green jacket, too. Amy is wearing _____ black shoes.

2. Amy is going to a party. She's wearing _____ blue dress with _____ white belt. Amy is wearing _____ white sandals. She is taking _____ white sweater to wear if she is cold.

3. Amy is at home. She's wearing comfortable clothing. Amy is wearing

_____

_____

_____

☀ The Clothing Store

A. Complete.

1. How much __is__ __this__ hat?   __It's__ $15.

2. How much __are__ __these__ sandals?   __They're__ $20.

3. How much _____ _____ skirt?   _____ $28.

4. How much _____ _____ gloves?   _____ $17.

5. How much _____ _____ briefs?   _____ $7.

6. How much _____ _____ sweater?   _____ $30.

7. How much _____ _____ tie?   _____ $17.

8. How much _____ _____ shorts?   _____ $22.

B. Pair practice. Ask and answer questions about the price of each item. Put a price on the empty tags.

> How much is this belt?
>
> How much are these shoes?

> It's sixteen dollars.
>
> They're thirty-seven dollars.

C. Read and practice.

Clerk: Hello. Can I help you?

Customer: Yes, I'm looking for a shirt.

Clerk: What size?

Customer: Medium.

Clerk: Our shirts are here.

Customer: I like this shirt.

Clerk: Try it on. The mirror is over there.

Customer: I like it. How much is it?

Clerk: It's $50. But today it's on sale for $35.

Customer: Great. I'll take it.

D. Write a conversation between a clerk and a customer.

> Be careful! Look at the changes for singular and plural in the conversation.

Clerk: Hello. _____.

Customer: Yes, I'm looking for _____.

Clerk: What size?

Customer: _____.

Clerk: Our _____ are here.

Customer: I like **this / these** _____.

Clerk: Try **it / them** on. The mirror is over there.

Customer: I like **it / them**. How much _____?

Clerk: _____ $_____, but today _____ on sale for $_____.

Customer: Great. I'll take **it / them**.

The Weather: Dictionary

A. Listen and repeat.

Weather

It's sunny.

It's cloudy.

It's windy.

It's raining.

It's snowing.

It's foggy.

It's hot.

It's warm.

It's cool.

It's cold.

Seasons

spring

summer

fall

winter

B. Listen to the weather. Find the city and write the temperature on the map.

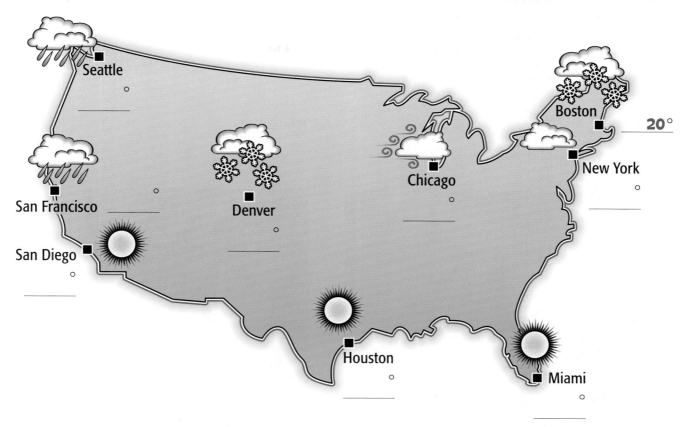

C. Write the weather conditions from the map above.

1. It's _____snowing and cold_____ in Boston.

2. It's _____ in New York.

3. It's _____ in Miami.

4. It's _____ in Houston.

5. It's _____ in San Diego.

6. It's _____ in San Francisco.

7. It's _____ in Seattle.

8. It's _____ in Denver.

9. It's _____ in Chicago.

| cold |
| cloudy |
| raining |
| windy |
| snowing |
| hot |
| warm |
| cool |
| cold |

Working Together

A. Sit in a group. Discuss these pictures.

1. Where are these people?
2. What are they doing?
3. What season is it? What's the weather?
4. What is each person wearing?

B. What are they wearing? Describe two classmates. Describe your teacher. What are they wearing?

Juan is wearing blue jeans and a black T-shirt. He's wearing sneakers and socks. On his desk, Juan has a white Yankee baseball cap.

C. Get dressed! Dress Roberto. Don't show your picture to your partner. Describe Roberto's clothing. Can your partner draw him?

Put some clothes on Roberto!
Describe your picture to your partner.

Listen to your partner.
Draw Roberto's clothes.

A. Listen. Circle the clothes Monica is going to buy.

coat	dress	gloves	skirt
sneakers	sweater	hat	socks

B. Circle Yes or No.

1. Monica is in the clothing store.   Yes   No

2. Monica is shopping alone.   Yes   No

3. It's cold now.   Yes   No

4. Monica likes the coat she is trying on.   Yes   No

5. Monica is going to spend a lot of money today.   Yes   No

6. Monica needs winter clothes.   Yes   No

7. Monica was in the United States last winter.   Yes   No

8. It's hot all year in Boston.   Yes   No

C. Complete.

1. Monica is from _____Cuba_____.

2. She came to the United States in _____.

3. She lives in _____.

4. In Boston, it is hot in the _____.

5. In Boston, it is cold in the _____.

6. In January, it is going to _____.

7. In Cuba, the weather is _____.

8. Right now, Monica is in a _____.

9. The _____ is 30°.

10. It's very _____ outside now.

Boston
winter
cold
snow
clothing store
temperature
May
summer
✓Cuba
hot

D. Check the tense.

	Past	Present	Future
1. The coat is $60.	☐	✓	☐
2. Monica lives in Boston.	☐	☐	☐
3. Monica lived in Cuba last year.	☐	☐	☐
4. It's going to snow in January.	☐	☐	☐
5. Monica is going to buy a sweater.	☐	☐	☐
6. Monica came to the United States last May.	☐	☐	☐
7. It's 30 degrees outside.	☐	☐	☐
8. It was sunny and hot in the summer.	☐	☐	☐
9. Monica is going to buy a hat.	☐	☐	☐
10. Monica needs warm clothes.	☐	☐	☐

E. In your notebook, write about Monica at the clothing store.

Reading: Climate Zones

A. Before You Read. Look at the map. What zone do you live in?

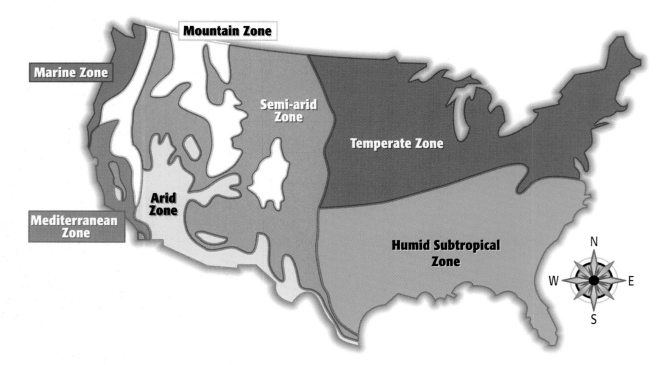

Mountain Zone

Marine Zone

Semi-arid Zone

Temperate Zone

Arid Zone

Mediterranean Zone

Humid Subtropical Zone

N W E S

The United States is very large, so it has many kinds of weather. There are seven climate zones in the United States. The **temperate** zone is in the north. There are four seasons. The summers are warm and humid, and the winters are cold, with four or five snowstorms. The **humid subtropical** zone has long, hot summers. The winters are short and can have a lot of rain. These areas can receive 60" of rain a year. The **mountain** zone has a long, cold winter with heavy snow. Some areas receive over 200" of snow a year. A large part of the Southwest is **arid** or **semi-arid**. These areas are very dry. There are many large deserts. The West Coast is in two climate zones. In the **marine** zone, there are long, cool summers and mild winters. There is often fog and light rain. In the **Mediterranean** area in the south, the summers are long and dry. The winters are rainy and mild.

B. Complete.

1. The ____Mediterranean____ zone has mild winters with a lot of rain.
2. The _____ zone has long, cold winters with heavy snow.
3. The _____ zone has fog and light rain all year.
4. The _____ zone has very dry weather all year.
5. The _____ zone has long, hot summers.
6. I live in the _____ zone. The weather is _____.

Writing Our Stories:
Weather

A. Read.

PUERTO RICO
San Juan

I live in Virginia. We have four seasons. The summer is long and hot, and the winter is mild. It doesn't snow very often. Right now, it's spring, my favorite season. The days are warm, and the nights are cool. I usually wear jeans and a shirt.

I am from Puerto Rico. The climate is hot and tropical. It is sunny and hot almost every day. The fall is hurricane season, and we sometimes have bad storms with heavy wind and rain. But most of the time, the weather is beautiful.

B. Complete these sentences.

I live in _____. We have _____ seasons.

The weather is _____

_____.

Right now, it's _____.

I am from _____. We have _____ seasons.

The weather is _____

_____.

Writing Note

Names of states and countries begin with a capital letter.

C. In your notebook, write about the weather in your area. What is the weather in your country?

Practicing on Your Own

A. Answer.

What is So Jung wearing?

1. _____

2. _____

3. _____

4. _____

What is Victor wearing?

1. _____

2. _____

3. _____

4. _____

B. Answer.

Yes, it is.
No, it isn't.

1. Is it raining in Boston?   _____

2. Is it snowing in Boston?   _____

3. Is it cold there?   _____

4. Is it hot in Houston?   _____

5. Is it sunny in Houston?   _____

6. Is it going to rain there?   _____

7. Is it cool in Seattle?   _____

8. Is it cloudy in Seattle?   _____

9. Is it going to rain there?   _____

C. What is the weather in your area today?

_____

Looking at Numbers

A. Figure it out!

1. Monica is buying a red coat for $75. Her hat is $15, and her gloves are $20. How much is she going to spend?

2. Monica is buying a hat for her sister. It's $17. Monica is giving the clerk $50. How much is her change?

3. Monica likes a blue sweater. It is $60, but it's on sale for 50% off. How much is the sweater?

4. Monica is trying on a red dress. It's $40. All the dresses in the store are 10% off today. How much is the dress?

5. Monica bought a lot of clothes. She has only $50 in her wallet. She likes some black boots. They are $90, but they're on sale today for half price. Can she buy the boots?

Grammar Summary

▶ **1. Present continuous**	
I **am wearing** a cap.	
He **is wearing** a sweater.	
She **is wearing** sneakers.	
▶ **2. *How much* questions**	
How much is this shirt?	It's $34.
How much are these briefs?	They're $8.
▶ **3. Short questions and answers**	
Is it cold in Alaska?	Yes, it **is.**
Is it cold in Arizona?	No, it **isn't.**

11 Food

 Dictionary: Breakfast, Lunch, Dinner, Beverages, Dessert, Fruit

 A. Listen and repeat.

Breakfast

eggs

cereal

pancakes

bacon

toast

donut

bagel

Lunch

hamburger

french fries

salad

soup

turkey sandwich

tuna salad sandwich

lettuce

tomato

cucumber

Dinner

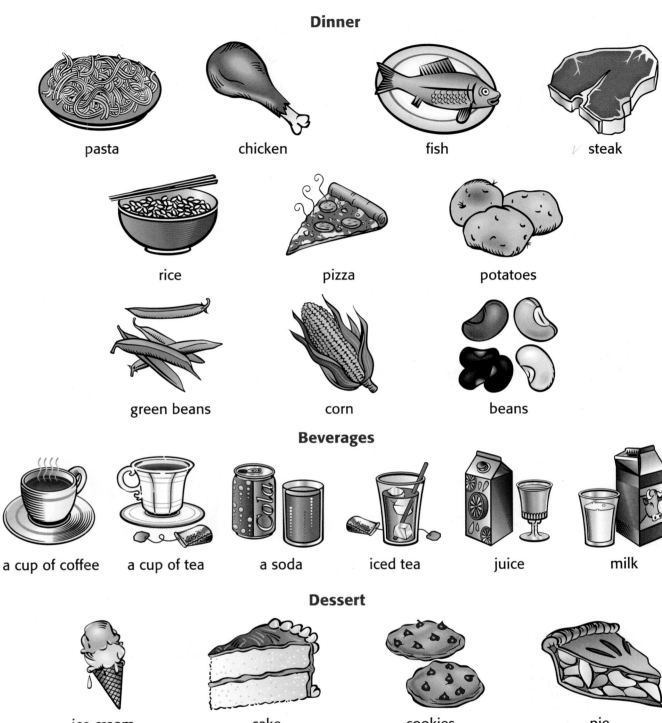

pasta

chicken

fish

steak

rice

pizza

potatoes

green beans

corn

beans

Beverages

a cup of coffee

a cup of tea

a soda

iced tea

juice

milk

Dessert

ice cream

cake

cookies

pie

Fruit

bananas

an apple

oranges

grapes

mangoes

Active Grammar: Present Tense

A. Complete. What do you like to eat? Look at the dictionary. Write five foods that you like. Write five foods that you don't like.

I like . . .

1. _____
2. _____
3. _____
4. _____
5. _____

I don't like . . .

6. _____
7. _____
8. _____
9. _____
10. _____

B. Listen. What does he eat?

Breakfast

Time: __7__ : __15__

He eats ___a bagel___ and ___fruit___.

He drinks _____.

Lunch

Time: ____ : ____ to ____ : ____

He eats _____ and

_____.

He drinks _____.

For dessert, he has _____.

Dinner

Time: ____ : ____

He eats _____, _____, and _____.

He drinks _____.

C. Complete. What do you eat for breakfast?

1. What time do you eat breakfast?

   I eat breakfast at _____ : _____.

2. What do you eat for breakfast?

   I eat _____

   _____.

3. What time do you eat lunch?

   I eat lunch at _____ : _____.

4. What do you eat for lunch?

   I eat _____.

5. What time do you eat dinner?

   I eat dinner at _____ : _____.

6. What do you eat for dinner?

   I eat _____.

Culture Note
Americans usually eat three meals a day. The biggest meal is dinner.

D. The typical food of my country. Make a list of the typical foods in your country. Compare with a partner.

Breakfast	Lunch	Dinner
_____	_____	_____
_____	_____	_____
_____	_____	_____

Dessert	Fruit	Beverages
_____	_____	_____
_____	_____	_____
_____	_____	_____

E. Complete with *always, sometimes,* or *never.*

Always = 100%
Sometimes = 50%
Never = 0%

1. I _____ eat breakfast.

2. I _____ drink juice at breakfast.

3. I _____ drink coffee in the morning.

4. I _____ eat lunch.

5. I _____ eat dinner with my family.

6. I _____ drink coffee at night.

7. I _____ prepare my own meals.

8. I _____ eat at restaurants.

9. I _____ eat fast food.

F. Answer.

1. Do you eat fast food?

2. Do you like fast food?

3. Give an example of a fast-food restaurant.

4. Is fast food good for your health?

5. What kind of food do children like?

6. Which do you like more, fast food or food cooked at home?

Culture Note

Fast food is food that is prepared quickly. Hamburgers and hot dogs are two fast foods.

G. Complete and compare your answers with a partner.

1. My favorite food is _____.

2. My favorite drink is _____.

3. My favorite restaurant is _____.

4. My favorite fast-food restaurant is _____.

5. My favorite dessert is _____.

 Ordering Lunch

A. Read the menu.

LUNCH MENU

SANDWICHES	
Tuna salad sandwich	$5.25
Turkey sandwich	$5.25
Roast beef sandwich	$5.75
Hamburger	$4.00
Cheeseburger	$4.50
Hot dog	$2.25
French fries	$1.25

SALADS	
Small green salad	$2.75
Large green salad	$4.00
Chef's salad	$6.50

SOUPS	
Vegetable Soup	$2.00
Soup of the day	$2.50

BEVERAGES	
Coffee, tea	$ .75
Iced tea	$1.00
Soda	$ .75
Milkshake	$2.50

DESSERTS	
Ice cream	$1.50
Pie	$2.50

 B. What'll you have? Listen and write the order.

Woman: I'll have _____

_____ .

Man: I'll have _____

_____ .

C. Read and practice.

Waiter: What'll you have today?

Customer: I'll have a turkey sandwich on whole wheat toast.

Waiter: Lettuce and tomato?

Customer: Lettuce, but no tomato.

Waiter: Anything to drink?

Customer: I'll have iced tea, please.

> Bread
> white
> whole wheat
> rye
> a roll

Pronunciation: 'll

 A. Pronunciation. Listen and complete. Then, listen and repeat.

1. _____I'll have_____ a salad.

2. _____She'll have_____ a cup of tea.

3. _____He'll have_____ a hamburger.

4. _____ a small soda.

5. _____ a glass of juice.

6. _____ pancakes.

7. _____ a cheese pizza.

8. _____ pasta.

 Practice the sentences with a partner.

 Containers

A. Listen and repeat.

a can of soda   a glass of milk   a cup of coffee   a bottle of juice

B. Put the drinks in the correct columns on page 159. You may put a drink in more than one column.

soda

chocolate milk

iced coffee

espresso

hot chocolate

orange juice

milk

✓coffee

water

lemonade

iced tea

tea

a can of	a bottle of	a cup of	a glass of
		coffee	

Working Together

A. Pair practice. Sit with a partner. Ask questions and check (✓) the answers.

	Yes	No
Do you like hamburgers?		
Do you like hot dogs?		
Do you like chicken?		
Do you like rice?		
Do you like fish?		
Do you like vegetables?		

B. Complete the sentences about you and your partner.

1. I _____ hamburgers.

2. I _____ chicken.

3. I _____ rice.

4. My partner _____ hot dogs.

5. My partner _____ fish.

6. My partner _____ vegetables.

7. I _____ .

Present Tense
I like pizza.
I don't like chicken.

He likes pizza.
He doesn't like beans.

She likes chicken.
She doesn't like rice.

C. In a group of three students, decide the prices on the menu.

DINNER MENU

PASTA		SOUPS	
Spaghetti with meat sauce.......................$		Onion Soup............................$	
		Soup of the day....................$	

MEAT, FISH, AND CHICKEN		BEVERAGES	
Hamburger/Cheeseburger special...........$		Coffee, tea............................$	
Chicken..$		Soda......................................$	
Steak...$		Milk.......................................$	
Fish..$			

SALADS		DESSERTS	
Small green salad.................................$		Ice cream.............................$	
		Cheesecake..........................$	

D. Read and practice the conversation.

Waiter:	Are you ready to order?
Customer 1:	Yes, we are.
Waiter:	What'll you have?
Customer 1:	I'll have onion soup and spaghetti with meat sauce.
Waiter:	Anything to drink?
Customer 1:	I'll have coffee.
Waiter:	And you? What'll you have?
Customer 2:	I'll have the cheeseburger special.
Waiter:	Would you like a salad?
Customer 2:	No, thank you.
Waiter:	Anything to drink?
Customer 2:	I'll have a diet soda.

E. Sit in a group of three students. Complete the conversation.

Waiter: Are you ready to order?

Customer 1: Yes, we are.

Waiter: What'll you have?

Customer 1: I'll have _____.

Waiter: Anything to drink?

Customer 1: I'll have _____.

Waiter: And you? What'll you have?

Customer 2: I'll have _____.

Waiter: Anything to drink?

Customer 2: _____

Waiter: _____

Culture Note

In the United States, Americans leave a tip for the waiter or waitress. Waiters and waitresses do not receive large salaries, so tips are important. People usually leave 15% of the check total.

F. Sit in a group. Talk and complete.

My Community

1. A good Chinese restaurant in my area is _____.

2. A good Mexican restaurant in my area is _____.

3. A good Italian restaurant in my area is _____.

4. A good pizzeria in my area is _____.

5. A good _____ restaurant in my area is _____.

The Big Picture: At Mario's Italian Restaurant

A. Listen.

B. Listen again and write the names on the correct person.

| Troy | Emma | Faye | Bob | Ann | Lori | Matthew |

C. Read and circle.

1. It's Saturday night.   Yes   (No)
2. Troy and Emma eat at Mario's on Friday nights.   Yes   No
3. Troy and Emma like to sit by the door.   Yes   No
4. Faye always works on Fridays.   Yes   No
5. Faye is a good waitress.   Yes   No
6. Troy and Emma are good customers.   Yes   No
7. Troy and Emma are ordering pasta.   Yes   No

D. Read and circle.

1. Who is sitting next to the window?

   (a.) Troy and   **b.** Bob and   **c.** Faye is.   **d.** Lori is.
   Emma are.   Ann are.

2. When do Troy and Emma eat at Mario's?

   a. Every day.   **b.** Every night.   **c.** On Fridays.   **d.** Italian.

3. Why do Troy and Emma sit at Faye's table?

   a. Because they like the food.   **c.** Because they're hungry.

   b. Because they like her.

4. When do Bob and Ann like to eat out?

   a. On Fridays.   **b.** Every   **c.** Every   **d.** Every
                         weekend.   night.   morning.

5. Why are Bob and Ann eating out tonight?

   a. Because they're hungry.   **c.** Because they're tired.

   b. Because they like to cook.

E. Complete.

1. Troy and Emma _____are eating_____ at Mario's.
2. They _____ at Faye's table.
3. Emma _____ at the menu.
4. Troy _____ a salad and chicken.
5. Faye _____ Troy's and Emma's orders.
6. Bob's family _____ pizza.
7. They _____ soda.

| is ordering |
| are sitting |
| is eating |
| ✓are eating |
| are drinking |
| is taking |
| is looking |

Reading: Pizza Delivery

A. Before You Read.

1. Do you like pizza?

2. Where do you eat pizza?

3. What toppings do you like on your pizza?

Clerk:	Hello, Buona Pizza. May I take your order?
Customer:	Hello, I'd like to order a large pizza.
Clerk:	What toppings do you want on it?
Customer:	Pepperoni and green pepper.
Clerk:	OK. A large pizza with pepperoni and green peppers. That's $8.50. What's your address?
Customer:	1516 Central Avenue.
Clerk:	What's your phone number?
Customer:	555-6644.
Clerk:	OK. Thank you.
Customer:	How long will it take?
Clerk:	Thirty minutes. It's Friday, and we're always busy on Fridays.
Customer:	OK. Thank you. Good-bye.
Clerk:	Thank you for calling Buona Pizza.

B. Complete.

1. What size pizza did the customer order? _____

2. How many toppings did the customer order? _____

3. What toppings did the customer order? _____

4. It's 7:00. What time will the pizza arrive? _____

Writing Our Stories: Home Cooking

A. Read.

I live with my parents. My mother is a good cook, and we always eat dinner together. We are from Italy, and we like fresh Italian food. My mother shops in the afternoon. She usually buys cheese, pasta, bread, meat, and fresh vegetables. For dinner, we always have pasta, a little meat, and a vegetable. We always have salad. We all drink water with our meal. Everything is delicious!

B. Complete the sentences or circle the answers.

1. I live _____.

2. _____ **cook / cooks** _____.

3. We **always / sometimes / never** eat meals together.

4. I am from _____.

5. _____ _____ at _____.
   shop/shops   supermarket

6. For dinner, I have _____.

7. I drink _____.

8. For dessert, I have _____.

> **Writing Note**
> Use commas in a list of three or more people, places or things: cheese, pasta, bread, and meat.

C. In your notebook, write about meals at your home.

A. Complete.

1. I like _____ for breakfast.

2. I sometimes eat _____ for breakfast.

3. I always drink _____ at breakfast time.

4. I never eat _____ for breakfast.

5. I like _____ or _____ for lunch.

6. I sometimes eat _____ or _____ for dinner.

7. I sometimes eat _____ for dessert.

8. I don't like _____.

B. Put this conversation in order. Then write the conversation.

_6_   **Customer:**   I'll have a large soda.

_2_   **Customer:**   Yes, I am.

_3_   **Waitress:**   What'll you have?

_1_   **Waitress:**   Are you ready to order?

_5_   **Waitress:**   Anything to drink?

_4_   **Customer:**   I'll have a small cheese pizza.

Waitress: _Are you ready to order?_ _____

Customer: _____

Waitress: _____

Customer: _____

Waitress: _____

Customer: _____

Looking at Numbers

A. What is the total for each bill? How much tip will you leave?

Hill's Diner

Scrambled Eggs	$3.00
Juice	.75
Coffee	.75
Total	4.50

45
22.50
68

Mario's Italian Restaurant

2 salads	$8.00
Spaghetti	9.50
Chicken	12.50
2 coffees	2.50
Total	32.50

3.25
1.63
4.88

Grammar Summary

▶ 1. Present tense

I **like** chicken.

I **don't like** fish.

He **likes** mangoes.

He **doesn't like** bananas.

▶ 2. Adverbs of frequency

I **always** drink water.

I **sometimes** drink coffee.

I **never** drink soda.

She **always** eats a small breakfast.

She **sometimes** eats a big lunch.

She **never** eats a big dinner.

▶ 3. *Will / 'll*

I'll have the chicken.

He'll have the fish.

She'll have the turkey.

We'll have a pizza.

They'll have hamburgers.

Finding an Apartment

Dictionary: Adjectives, Inside the Apartment, Apartment Problems

A. Listen and repeat.

Adjectives

sunny

dark

clean

dirty

quiet

noisy

near / close to

far from

Inside the Apartment

faucet

freezer
refrigerator

heater / radiator

stove
oven

lights

electricity

lock

air conditioner

ceiling

Apartment Problems

The faucet is leaking.

The paint is peeling.

The air conditioner isn't working.

The stove isn't working.

The lights aren't working.

The freezer is broken.

The lock is broken.

The heat is off.

The electricity is off.

The window is stuck.

There's a mouse.

There are cockroaches.

Active Grammar: Present Continuous

A. Listen and (circle.)

1. Yes, there is.   No, there isn't.
2. Yes, there are.   No, there aren't.
3. Yes, there are.   No, there aren't.
4. Yes, there is.   No, there isn't.
5. Yes, there is.   No, there isn't.
6. Yes, there is.   No, there isn't.
7. Yes, there is.   No, there isn't.

B. Sit in a group of three or four students. Talk about the apartment.

> **There is / There are**
> There is a large kitchen.
> There are two bedrooms.

C. Listen and write.

1. The _____ is peeling.
2. The _____ is leaking.
3. A _____ is stuck.
4. The _____ is off.
5. The _____ are noisy.
6. The _____ is off.
7. There is a _____ in the apartment.

D. Check (✓) and discuss: How did you find your apartment?

☐ I asked a friend.
☐ I looked in the newspaper.
☐ I saw a sign on a building.

What's the best way to find an apartment?

☀ Reading the Classified Ads

A. Listen and repeat.

air conditioner	elevator	parking
apartment	furnished	pets
basement	included	security deposit
bath	large	transportation
bathroom	location	utilities
bedroom	modern	washer/dryer
carpeting		

Pets

B. Read and complete with a partner.

> What does *apt.* mean?

apt.
a/c
BR
bsmt.
lge.
loc.
mod.
elev.
incl.
sec. dep.
utils.

1. Apt. means ___apartment___.
2. A/C means _____.
3. BR means _____.
4. Bsmt. means _____.
5. Lge. means _____.
6. Loc. means _____.
7. Mod. means _____.
8. Elev. means _____.
9. Incl. means _____.
10. Sec. dep. means _____.
11. Utils. means _____.

C. Pronunciation. Listen. How many syllables do you hear?

1. elevator ___4___
2. utility ___4___
3. utilities ___4___
4. apartment ___3___
5. neighborhood ___3___
6. transportation ___4___
7. superintendent ___5___
8. electricity ___5___
9. air conditioner ___5___
10. neighbor ___2___
11. basement ___2___
12. included ___3___

Practice the words above with a partner.

E. Read and complete.

For Rent
Lge. 1 BR, w/ nice kitchen, sunny,
elev. building w/ new windows, quiet,
new carpet, no pets, utils. include,
near trans., sec. dep., $625/mo.

1. The apartment is ____large____ .

2. It's _____ .

3. There are _____ .

4. It has _____ .

5. There is a _____ .

6. The rent is _____ .

F. Read and circle.

> 2 BR sunny apt., lge., new
> carpeting, utils. incl., 1 1/2 bath,
> no pets, sec. dep.: $940

1. Yes (No) The apartment has three bedrooms.

2. Yes No Utilities are included.

3. Yes No You can have a pet.

> 3 lge. rooms, heat, hot water incl.
> Excellent loc., parking: $650

4. Yes No The rooms are large.

5. Yes No Electricity is included.

6. Yes No The apartment is in a good location.

> Family house, 3 BR, 2 baths, liv.
> rm., hot water incl., parking, small
> pets ok, near transportation: $1700

7. Yes No The house has a dining room.

8. Yes No All utilities are included.

9. Yes No All pets are okay in this house.

G. Write a classified ad for your house or apartment.

H. Match.

1. How many bedrooms are there?   a. It's $540 a month.

2. Where is the apartment? e   b. No. No pets are allowed.

3. Can I have a dog? b   c. Yes, a bus stop is on the corner.

4. Is it near transportation? c   d. There are two bedrooms.

5. How much is the rent? a   e. It's on Hope Street, near the bank.

 Calling the Super

super = superintendent

A. **Listen. Match the conversation and the problem. Then (circle) the time.**

	Problem	When will the super be here?		
a. _____	The lock is broken.	Right away	Later today	Tomorrow
b. _____	The faucet is leaking.	Right away	Later today	Tomorrow
c. _____	The stove isn't working.	Right away	Later today	Tomorrow
d. __1__	The air conditioner isn't working.	(Right away)	Later today	Tomorrow
e. _____	There's a mouse in the kitchen.	Right away	Later today	Tomorrow
f. _____	There's a leak in the ceiling.	Right away	Later today	Tomorrow

B. **Pair practice. Describe the problem to the super.**

What's the problem?

The sink is leaking.

Working Together: Your Apartment

A. Interview two students about their apartments.

Questions	Partner 1: _____		Partner 2: _____	
1. Is your apartment sunny?	Yes	No	Yes	No
2. Are there two bedrooms in your apartment?	Yes	No	Yes	No
3. Is your kitchen large?	Yes	No	Yes	No
4. Is your apartment near transportation?	Yes	No	Yes	No
5. Is your apartment noisy?	Yes	No	Yes	No
6. Is your apartment close to school?	Yes	No	Yes	No
7. Is there an elevator in your building?	Yes	No	Yes	No
8. Is your neighborhood safe at night?	Yes	No	Yes	No

B. Complete about the interview.

1. _____'s apartment **is / isn't** sunny.
   _{Partner 1}
2. **His / Her** apartment has _____ bedrooms.
3. **His / Her** kitchen **is / isn't** large.
4. **His / Her** apartment **is / isn't** near transportation.
5. **His / Her** apartment _____.
6. _____'s apartment **is / isn't** noisy.
   _{Partner 2}
7. **His / Her** apartment has _____ bedrooms.
8. **His / Her** apartment **is / isn't** close to school.
9. **His / Her** neighborhood **is / isn't** safe at night.
10. **His / Her** apartment _____.

C. Talk about the apartments with your partners. Do they like their apartments? Why or why not?

D. Read and practice.

A: Hello, I'm calling about the one-bedroom apartment.

B: Well, it's a nice apartment, and it's sunny.

A: Does the rent include utilities?

B: It includes heat and hot water.

A: Is the apartment near transportation?

B: Yes, it's near the bus stop.

A: Is there an elevator in the building?

B: No, there isn't.

A: When can I see the apartment?

B: You can see it tomorrow morning.

Culture Note

In the United States, people often have to make appointments to look at an apartment.

E. Complete with a partner.

A: Hello, I'm calling about the _____ apartment.

B: Well, it's a _____ apartment, and it's _____.

A: Does the rent include utilities?

B: It includes _____.

A: Is the apartment near _____?

B: _____.

A: Is there _____ in the building?

B: _____.

A: When can I see the apartment?

B: You can see it _____.

F. Act out your conversation.

The Big Picture: My Neighborhood

◀♦ **A. Listen.**

B. Read and circle.

1.	The apartment is on the fourth floor.	Yes	No
2.	The bedroom is small.	Yes	No
3.	Ana has a cat.	Yes	No
4.	Ana likes her neighborhood.	Yes	No
5.	The telephone company is next to her apartment building.	Yes	No
6.	Ana works at the post office.	Yes	No
7.	Ana takes the bus to work.	Yes	No
8.	Ana likes her neighbors.	Yes	No

C. Read and complete.

1. There is __a__ ____bedroom____ in the apartment.

2. There is a _____ in the apartment.

3. There are _____ in the apartment.

4. There isn't an _____ in the building.

5. There aren't any _____ in the building.

6. There's a _____ down the street.

7. There is a _____ next to the building.

8. The _____ are quiet and friendly.

bank
✓ bedroom
elevator
kitchen
neighbors
parking lot
pets
windows

D. Complete.

1. The laundromat is ____next to____ Ana's building.

2. The park is _____ Ana's building.

3. The bus stop is _____ Ana's building.

4. The bus stop is _____ the post office and the library.

5. The market is _____ the school.

6. The parking lot is _____ Ana's building.

7. The bank is _____ the telephone company.

8. The laundromat is _____ Ana's building and the market.

across from
between
next to

E. Pair practice. Where does she ... ?

buy fruit
cash her check
get books
pay the telephone bill
wash her clothes
work

Where does she work?

She works at the school.

school

laundromat

supermarket

bookstore

telephone company

bank

Reading: Walter the Exterminator

A. Before You Read.

1. Do you live in an apartment or a house?

2. What is an exterminator?

3. Do you ever need an exterminator?

4. How do you say *cockroach* in your language?

If you live in an apartment or a house, sometimes you need an exterminator. The exterminator goes into a house, apartment, or office building when there is a problem with ants, mice, or roaches.

Walter is an exterminator. He has a pest control business and 26 years of experience. He and his four employees work in private homes. His wife does the office work. Walter gets ten to twelve calls per day. He likes his job. He likes to talk to the different customers. He especially likes to eliminate pests.

Walter's most common calls are about mice and ants. When Walter gets a call, he goes to the home. For many insects, he sprays insecticide in small spaces. For mice, he puts out traps or poison. When there are no more pests in the house, Walter is happy. Then he goes to the next home to find the next pest.

B. Underline and number the answers in the reading.

1. Where does Walter work?

2. Who does the office work for Walter?

3. How many calls does he get per day?

4. Why does Walter like his job?

5. What is the most common problem for Walter's customers?

6. How does Walter feel when there are no more pests in the house?

Writing Our Stories:
My Apartment

A. Read.

My name is José. I live in a sunny one-bedroom apartment with my brother. We live on the first floor. Our building has three floors. Our building doesn't have an elevator. My brother sleeps on the pull-out sofa in the *sofa bed* living room. We have a small kitchen and a living room. The rent is a little expensive, but our apartment is in a safe neighborhood, and our neighbors are very friendly. We need a bigger apartment with two bedrooms. We also need more space for our computer.

B. Check (✓) the true sentences about your apartment or house.

☐ **1.** My apartment is sunny.
☐ **2.** My apartment has two bedrooms.
☐ **3.** My kitchen is large.
☐ **4.** I have a living room.
☐ **5.** My building has an elevator.
☐ **6.** My apartment is in a safe neighborhood.
☐ **7.** My rent is cheap.
☐ **8.** My neighbors are friendly.

C. In your notebook, write about your apartment or house.

Writing Note
Check your punctuation. Begin each sentence with a capital letter. End each sentence with a period.

Practicing on Your Own

A. Read and complete.

1. The lock is _____broken_____.

2. There is a _____ in the hallway.

3. The air _____ _____ _____.

4. The paint _____ _____.

5. The apartment is _____.

6. There _____ two _____ in the apartment.

7. The apartment isn't _____.

B. Look at the map of a neighborhood. Complete each question and answer.

1. __Is__ __there__ a bus stop near the apartment?   Yes, there __is__.

2. _____ there a bank _____ the neighborhood?   No, there _____.

3. Is the laundromat _____ _____ the library?   No, it _____.

4. Is _____ a bookstore in the neighborhood?   Yes, _____ _____.

5. Is the apartment building _____ the park?   Yes, _____ _____.

6. _____ there any parking lots in the neighborhood?   Yes, _____.

180   UNIT 12

Looking at Forms: The Bottom Part of a Lease

A. Complete.

Lease

_____	_____	_____
Last Name	First Name	MI
_____	_____	_____
Spouse's Last Name	First Name	MI

Number of Occupants _____*
*No more than 5 occupants in one apartment

_____	_____	_____
Place of Employment	City	State

_____ Year of Employment   Occupation _____

References

_____ (___) _____
Name of Reference (Not a relative)   Tel.

_____ _____
Name of Bank   Address   Account Number

_____	_____	_____	_____
Signature of tenant	Date	Signature of spouse	Date

Grammar Summary

▶ 1. Present continuous

The faucet **is leaking.**

The air conditioner **isn't working.**

The lights **aren't working.**

▶ 2. *There is / There are*

There is a large kitchen.

Is there a large kitchen?   Yes, **there is.**

There are two bedrooms.

Are there three bedrooms?   No, **there aren't.**

▶ 3. Adjectives

The freezer is **broken.**   The window is **stuck.**

13 Applying for a Job

 Dictionary: Hotel Occupations

A. Listen and repeat.

Hotel Occupations

desk clerk

babysitter

busboy

cook

electrician

housekeeper

landscaper

laundry worker

manager

plumber

security guard

waiter / waitress

van driver /
airport shuttle driver

Active Grammar: Present Tense

A. Match.

_g_ 1. an airport shuttle driver   **a.** cleans and clears tables

_____ 2. a desk clerk   **b.** washes and dries sheets and towels

_____ 3. a babysitter   **c.** serves food

_____ 4. a waitress   **d.** takes reservations

_____ 5. a cook   **e.** repairs bathrooms

_____ 6. a laundry worker   **f.** is the supervisor

_____ 7. a housekeeper   **g.** drives a van

_____ 8. a manager   **h.** takes care of children

_____ 9. a plumber   **i.** prepares food

_____ 10. a busboy   **j.** cleans and vacuums rooms

B. Complete with a partner.

1. An _____airport shuttle driver_____ works outside.

2. A _____ wears a uniform.

3. A _____ needs English for the job.

4. A _____ doesn't need English for the job.

5. A _____ needs experience.

6. A _____ doesn't need experience.

7. A _____ gets tips.

8. A _____ has a boring job.

9. A _____ has an interesting job.

uniform

C. Complete the sentences about your present job.

1. I am a(n) _____ .

2. I _____ an interesting job.
   _{have / don't have}

3. I _____ English at work.
   _{speak / don't speak}

4. I _____ a uniform.
   _{wear / don't wear}

5. I _____ tips.
   _{get / don't get}

6. My job _____ experience.
   _{needs / doesn't need}

 D. Pair practice.

1. Does a cook wear a uniform?

2. Does a manager get tips?

3. Does a manager repair bathrooms?

4. Does a waitress serve food?

5. Does a housekeeper prepare food?

6. Does a babysitter take reservations?

7. Does a desk clerk stand all day?

8. Does an airport shuttle driver drive a van?

> Yes, she does. Yes, he does.
> No, she doesn't. No, he doesn't.

A. Listen to each person talk about his or her job experience. Write the number of the speaker under each picture.

_____

___1___

_____

_____

B. Check (✓) your job skills.

riding lawn mower

☐ **1.** I can speak a little English.
☐ **2.** I can speak English well.
☐ **3.** I can clean a room.
☐ **4.** I can operate a riding lawn mower.
☐ **5.** I can make drinks.
☐ **6.** I can cook different kinds of food.
☐ **7.** I can drive a car.
☐ **8.** I can drive a stick shift.
☐ **9.** I can use a computer.
☐ **10.** I can drive a truck.

stick shift

What else can you do?

I can _____.

I can _____.

 Job Experience

A. Listen and complete.

1. In my country, Colombia, I was a _____ _____ in a high school. Now I am a _____ _____ at a hotel. I am studying for my teaching certificate. I want to teach Spanish to high school students.

2. In my country, Poland, I was a _____ in a four-star hotel. Now I am a _____ in a small hotel. I can make reservations and use a computer. I am preparing for a management job.

3. In my country, Brazil, I was a _____ _____. Now I am a _____ in a hotel. I am studying English and dance at a community college. I can do the samba, salsa, and teach many dances. I want to get a degree.

B. Pronunciation: *was.* Listen and repeat.

1. I am a cook.   I was a cook.
2. I am a mechanic.   I was a mechanic.
3. He is a landscaper.   He was a landscaper.
4. She is a housewife.   She was a housewife.
5. He is a teacher.   He was a teacher.
6. She is a manager.   She was a manager.
7. I am a plumber.   I was a plumber.
8. He is a security guard. He was a security guard.

C. Listen and (circle) Now or Past.

1. Now (Past)
2. Now Past
3. Now Past
4. Now Past

5. Now Past
6. Now Past
7. Now Past
8. Now Past

D. Read.

Work Experience			
From	**To**	**Employer**	**Position**
1996	present	The Flamingo	assistant cook
1992	1996	Tio Pepe	head cook

Alex: I'm applying for a job as a cook.

Manager: Do you have any experience?

Alex: Yes, I am an assistant cook at the Flamingo in Tampa.

Manager: Any other experience?

Alex: I was the head cook at Tio Pepe in Mexico City from 1992 to 1996.

Manager: Do ~~have you~~ *you have* any references?

Alex: Yes, I do. You can call the head cook at the Flamingo, and I have a letter from the manager at Tio Pepe.

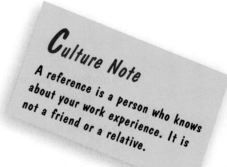

Culture Note

A reference is a person who knows about your work experience. It is not a friend or a relative.

 E. Practice the conversation with a partner.

F. Complete with your work experience.

Work Experience			
From	**To**	**Employer**	**Position**

 G. Tell a partner about your work experience.

 Job Ads

A. Read these job ads. Circle the jobs.

Help Wanted
Bellhop
Desk Clerk
Western Hotel
137 Kennedy Street
Apply in person.

Job Openings
Housekeepers
Laundry Workers
No Experience.
Will train on job.
Call the Carlton Hotel.
555-6777

Position Available
Cook
Experience Required
Paradise Hotel
Call 644-8899
Ask for Mr. Thomas.

Immediate Opening
Waiters and
Waitresses for
3-star New York Hotel
Restaurant
Experience required.
Apply in person.

Help Wanted
Landscaper
Experience with large
machines
Call Ms. Smith
At 433-1199.

Openings
Babysitter
2 references
Oceanside Hotel
Apply in person.

B. Sit with a partner. Write an ad for a job.

Help Wanted

_____

_____

_____

C. Read these classified ads from a newspaper. Check (✓) the information below.

FT = full time
PT = part time

Culture Note
A maintenance mechanic works in an office building or a hotel. The mechanic repairs anything that is not working.

COOK FT 2 years experience required. Excellent pay w/ benefits. Call Thurs. – Sat. 11:00 A.M. – 4:00 P.M. 555-2126

A

FRONT DESK CLERK for hotel PT Eve shift 3 P.M. – 11 P.M. Will train. Apply in person. Plaza Hotel. Seaside.

B

LANDSCAPER Immediate FT opening for landscape crew. Valid license required. $9.00/hour. Benefits, vacation. Call today. 555-9328

C

MAINTENANCE MECHANIC FT Must have painting, plumbing, and electrical skills. Salary based on experience. Good benefits. Sunrise Resort. 555-4334

D

	A	B	C	D
1. This job is full time.	☐	☐	✓	✓
2. This job pays $9.00 an hour.	☐	☐	☐	☐
3. This job has benefits.	☐	☐	☐	☐
4. This job requires a driver's license.	☐	☐	☐	☐
5. This job requires experience.	☐	☐	☐	☐
6. This job is from 3:00 P.M. to 11:00 P.M.	☐	☐	☐	☐
7. You can apply in person for this job.	☐	☐	☐	☐
8. You need to call about this job.	☐	☐	☐	☐
9. I would like to apply for this job.	☐	☐	☐	☐

 A Job Application

A. Read the information in Luis's application.

<table>
<tr><td colspan="4">Position _____valet_____</td><td>**The Sunrise Hotel**</td></tr>
</table>

Position _____valet_____   **The Sunrise Hotel**

Name _____Moreno_____ _____Luis_____ _____A._____
         Last   First   Middle

Address _____397_____ _____Marina Way_____ _____Largo_____ _____FL_____
        Number   Street   City   State

Social Security No. _333-55-0012_   Date of birth _6_ / _15_ / _80_

Telephone _555-6000_

Work Experience

From	To	Employer	Position
1999	present	Frank's Fried Chicken	cashier

Signature of applicant _____*Luis Moreno*_____

 B. Listen to the job interview. (Circle) *Yes* or *No*.

(Yes)	No	**1.**	Luis is interviewing for a job as a valet.
Yes	No	**2.**	He has experience as a valet.
Yes	No	**3.**	Luis has a clean driver's license.
Yes	No	**4.**	Luis had an accident last year.
Yes	No	**5.**	Luis can start tomorrow.
Yes	No	**6.**	This job is part time.
Yes	No	**7.**	The salary is $8.00 an hour.
Yes	No	**8.**	Luis will get tips.
Yes	No	**9.**	Luis can wear sneakers.

a valet

Working Together

 A. Pair work. Read and practice with a partner.

> **A:** I'm applying for a job as a security guard.
>
> **B:** Do you have any experience?
>
> **A:** Yes. I was a security guard at a bank in Atlantic City.
>
> **B:** When?
>
> **A:** From 1997 to 2002.
>
> **B:** We have an opening on the second shift, from 3:00 P.M. to 11:00 P.M.
>
> **A:** What is the salary?
>
> **B:** The salary is $7.50 an hour.
>
> **A:** Good.
>
> **B:** When can you start?
>
> **A:** I can start tomorrow.

Culture Note
Arrive five to ten minutes early for a job interview.

Culture Note
Many jobs have two or three shifts.
First shift:
7:00 A.M. to 3:00 P.M.
Second shift:
3:00 P.M. to 11:00 P.M.
Third shift:
11:00 P.M. to 7:00 A.M.

B. Write a conversation with a partner. One student is the manager. The other student is applying for a job.

C. Check (✓) and discuss: How did you find your job?

- ☐ A friend told me about the job.
- ☐ My relative works at the same place.
- ☐ I saw a Help Wanted sign at the company.
- ☐ I read about the job in the newspaper.
- ☐ I stopped at the factory and spoke to the manager.
- ☐ _____

What's a good way to find a job?

The Big Picture: The Sunrise Hotel

A. Listen and circle.

1.	Ricardo is the day manager of the Sunrise Hotel.	Yes	No
2.	The hotel has more than 200 rooms.	Yes	No
3.	The hotel has about 100 employees.	Yes	No
4.	The van driver parks cars.	Yes	No
5.	The hotel has three shifts.	Yes	No
6.	Night employees make more money than day employees.	Yes	No
7.	Everyone works full time.	Yes	No
8.	The salary is high.	Yes	No
9.	Many employees like the hours.	Yes	No
10.	The hotel has many job openings.	Yes	No

B. Listen. Who is the manager speaking to?

1. He's speaking to the _____housekeeper_____ .
2. He's speaking to the _____ .
3. He's speaking to the _____ .
4. He's speaking to the _____ .
5. He's speaking to the _____ .
6. He's speaking to the _____ .
7. He's speaking to the _____ .

> van driver
> waitress
> laundry worker
> ✓housekeeper
> desk clerk
> electrician
> valet

C. Complete.

is	earns	works	likes

1. Shelley _works_ at the Sunrise Hotel. She _is_ a desk clerk. She _works_ from 11:00 to 7:00. She _likes_ the hours because she can be home with her children in the daytime. She _earns_ $10.00 an hour.

2. Chin-Kun _____ at the Sunrise Hotel. He _____ a desk clerk. He _____ from 4:00 to 1:00 on Friday, Saturday, and Sunday. Chin-Kun _____ a teacher during the week. He _____ extra money on weekends at the hotel.

3. Kasia _____ a part-time waitress in the restaurant at the Sunrise Hotel. She _____ $4.00 an hour plus tips. She _____ the hours, but she doesn't like the pay. She _____ from 10:30 to 3:30 four days a week.

4. Fernando _____ part time as a busboy in the restaurant at the Sunrise Hotel. He _____ $3.00 an hour. He _____ from 6:00 to 10:30 on weekends. He _____ the hours because he _____ a college student, and he can take classes during the week.

Reading: The Ice Hotel

snow

ice

A. Before You Read.

1. Where is Sweden?

2. What's the weather in Sweden?

There's an unusual hotel in Jukkäsjarvi, Sweden. It's open only from the middle of December to late April. The name of the hotel is the Ice Hotel. The hotel is made completely of ice and snow. Every year, more and more visitors want to stay at this very cold hotel.

In the first year, the Ice Hotel had only one room. Now the hotel has 37 rooms and 6,500 overnight guests every year. The hotel has a reception desk, a main hall, a cinema, and hotel rooms. There's an ice church for weddings, too!

In early October, artists and workers prepare the hotel. They use special snow equipment to prepare snow and ice. In November, builders bring ice from a very clean river. In December, the outside of the hotel is finished.

The rooms are very quiet. There are no telephones and no televisions. The Ice Hotel visitors can use computers to send e-mail messages to friends and family.

In late April, the last guests leave the hotel. The weather becomes warmer, and the beautiful Ice Hotel begins to melt. In June, the Ice Hotel is a water hotel.

B. Circle T for true or F for false.

T **F** 1. There are many ice hotels in Sweden.

T F 2. The hotel is open for nine months a year.

T F 3. The hotel has 6,500 overnight guests a year.

T F 4. The hotel has a cinema, a church, and an exercise room.

T F 5. Builders begin preparing the hotel in April.

T F 6. The ice comes from a clean river.

T F 7. The hotel closes in December.

Writing Our Stories:
On the Job

A. Read.

I am a desk clerk at a small motel near a busy highway. The motel has 50 rooms. I like my job. I check people into the motel, and I check people out of the motel. I don't wear a uniform. I use a computer to type names and addresses. I like my boss. He is helpful. I like my hours, too. I work five days a week. My days off are Monday and Tuesday. I work from 3:00 P.M. to 11:00 P.M. I have a dinner break from 7:00 to 7:30. My salary is low, but the work is easy, and I like to talk to people. I don't work overtime. I have two sick days and one week of vacation.

B. Check (✓) the true sentences about your job.

_____ I have medical benefits.

_____ I have benefits for my family.

_____ I work overtime.

_____ I like my job.

_____ My hours are good.

_____ I work a shift.

_____ I like my hours.

_____ My co-workers are friendly.

C. In your notebook, write about your job.

Writing Note

Names of companies begin with capital letters: McDougal's, Astrosonic

Practicing on Your Own

A. Complete with *is* or *was*.

1. Michelle ____is____ a manager at the Sunrise Hotel. She has other experience as a manager. She _____ a manager in a large hotel from 1997 to 1999.

2. Rima has experience as a cook. She _____ a cook in an Italian restaurant from 1996 to 2000. Now she _____ the head cook at an Italian restaurant in Boston.

3. Frank _____ an experienced electrician. He _____ an electrician in his country from 1994 to 1999. Now he _____ the supervisor of electricians at the Sunrise Hotel.

B. Answer.

Yes, I do.
No, I don't.

1. Do you work at a hotel? _____

2. Do you work at night? _____

3. Do you wear a uniform? _____

4. Do you get tips? _____

5. Do you earn a good salary? _____

C. Complete.

likes   doesn't like

friendly
low
good
interesting
boring
helpful

1. Tony _____ his job because it is _____.

2. Henry _____ his co-workers because they are _____.

3. Julia _____ her job because the hours are _____.

4. Yumiko _____ her job because the salary is _____.

5. I **like / don't like** my job because it is _____.

Looking at Numbers

A. Figure it out!

1. Martin is a desk clerk. He makes $10.00 an hour. He works 40 hours a week. What is his weekly salary?

2. Tom is a plumber. He works 40 hours a week and makes $20.00 an hour. How much does he earn per week?

3. Myra works part time as a housekeeper. She earns $8.00 an hour. She works 15 hours a week. What is her weekly salary?

4. Tina is an airport shuttle driver. She makes $4.00 an hour. She works 10 hours a day, 5 days a week. She usually makes $70 a day in tips. How much does she make per day?

Grammar Summary

▶ **1. Present tense**

I **wear** a uniform.	I **don't wear** a uniform.
I **have** an interesting job.	I **don't have** an interesting job.
He **wears** a uniform.	He **doesn't wear** a uniform.
She **has** medical benefits.	She **doesn't have** medical benefits.

▶ **2. *Yes/No* questions**

Do you **like** your job?	Yes, I **do.**	No, I **don't.**
Does she **like** her job?	Yes, she **does.**	No, she **doesn't.**

▶ **3. Past *be***

I **am** a cook at the Flamingo.	(now)
I **was** a cook at Tio Pepe.	(past)
He **is** a plumber at a hotel.	(now)
He **was** a plumber at a motel.	(past)

▶ **4. *Can***

I **can drive** a van.	**Can** you **use** a computer?
He **can repair** equipment.	**Can** he **speak** English?
She **can cook** Italian food.	

A Visit to the Doctor

Dictionary: Parts of the Body, Health Problems, Remedies

A. Listen and repeat.

Parts of the Body

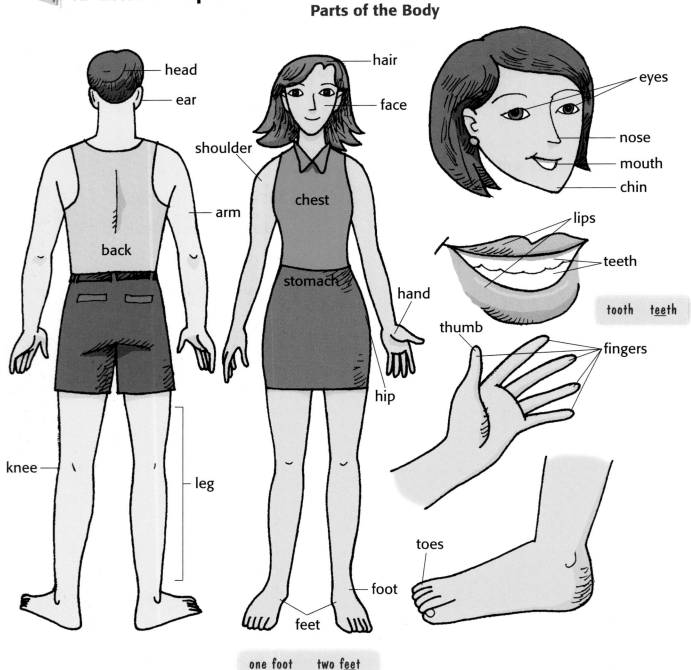

head
ear
shoulder
arm
back
knee
leg

hair
face
chest
stomach
hand
hip
foot
feet

eyes
nose
mouth
chin
lips
teeth

tooth   teeth

thumb
fingers

toes

one foot   two feet

Health Problems

allergy

asthma

burn

cold

chicken pox

cough

fever

headache

sore throat

stomachache

toothache

She's sneezing.

Remedies

aspirin

ibuprofen

ice pack

heating pad

inhaler

lotion

dentist

doctor

Active Grammar: *Have / Has*

A. Complete.

1.

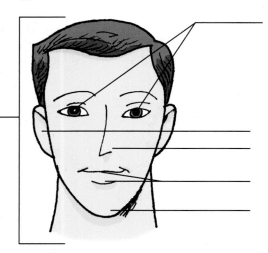

head	chin	eyes
ears	nose	lips

2.

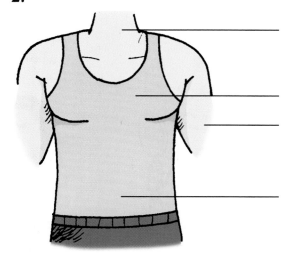

arm	chest
neck	stomach

3.

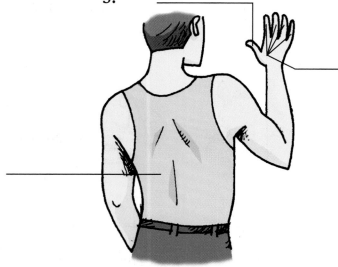

back	fingers	thumb

4.

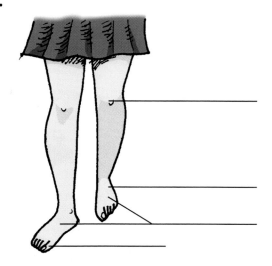

foot	feet	knee	toe

Where does it hurt?

 A. Listen and repeat.

1. Her __head__ hurts. 2. Her _____ hurts. 3. Her _____ hurts.

4. His _____ hurts. 5. His _____ hurts. 6. His _____ hurts.

 B. Listen again and write.

C. Listen and repeat.

> hurt = ache

| backache | earache | headache | stomachache | toothache |

D. Complete.

1. His tooth hurts.   He has a _____ toothache _____.
2. Her back hurts.   She has a _____.
3. My head hurts.   I have a _____.
4. His stomach hurts.   He has a _____.
5. My ear hurts.   I have an _____.

 Health Problems

Have / Has		
He She	has	a sore throat.
They	have	allergies.

A. Match.

1.

                She has the chicken pox.

2.

                She has a sore throat.

3.

                They have allergies.

4.

                They have colds.

5.

                He has a headache.

6.

                They have stomachaches.

7.

                He has asthma.

8.

                She has a fever.

Household Remedies

A. Listen and repeat.

1.    2.    3.    4.

5.    6.    7.    8.

B. Read and number.

_____ take aspirin   _____ drink liquids   _____ stay in bed

_____ call the doctor   _____ put on lotion   _____ use a heating pad

___1___ use an ice pack   _____ use an inhaler

C. Complete. What are they going to do?

> I am going to call the doctor.
> He is going to call the doctor.
> She is going to . . .
> They are going to . . .

call the dentist	stay in bed
call the doctor	✓take aspirin
drink some soda	take ibuprofen
drink hot tea	take some medicine
use an inhaler	use a heating pad

1. She has a headache. She is going to _____take aspirin_____.

2. They have sore throats. They are going to _____.

3. I have a backache. I'm going to _____.

4. She has a toothache. She's going to _____.

5. My son has asthma. He _____.

6. They have bad colds. They _____.

7. I have a fever. I _____.

 Reading Labels

A. Read the directions. (Circle) *must* or *must not*.

DIRECTIONS:
Adult Dose:
2 tsp. every 4 hours
Child Dose: 6 yrs.-12 yrs.:
1 tsp. every 4 hours
NOT FOR CHILDREN UNDER 6

My Community
Three drugstores in my area:
1. _____
2. _____
3. _____

1. Adults **(must)** / **must not** take two teaspoons every four hours.
2. Adults **must** / **(must not)** take four teaspoons every two hours.
3. Children under six **must** / **must not** take this medicine.

Directions:
Adults: Take 2 capsules every 4–6 hours.
Do not give to children.
Do not use with alcohol.

4. An adult **must** / **must not** take this medicine every four to six hours.
5. Parents **must** / **must not** give this medicine to children.
6. A patient **must** / **must not** drink alcohol and take this medicine.

Directions:
Take 1 capsule once a day.
Take with food or milk.

once a day = one time a day

7. A patient **must** / **must not** take one capsule once a day.
8. Patients **must** / **must not** take this medicine with food or milk.

Culture Note
To get a prescription, you must see a doctor.

Working Together: Who's your doctor?

A. Complete.

My doctor is _____.

My children's pediatrician is _____.

My dentist is _____.

My hospital is _____.

My pharmacy is _____.

> **Culture Note**
>
> Many doctors think that women and men forty years of age and older should have a full medical checkup (examination) once a year.

B. Match.

1. A pediatrician — checks my eyes.
2. An allergist — takes care of my children.
3. An obstetrician/gynecologist — helps me talk about my problems.
4. An optometrist — checks my skin.
5. A psychologist — takes care of women.
6. A dermatologist — helps me control my allergies.

C. Pair practice. Ask and answer questions about these health problems.

What do you do for a headache?

I take aspirin.

headache

a fever

chicken pox

an allergy

a stomachache

a bad cold

backache

a bad cough

call the dentist
call the doctor
drink soda
drink hot tea
put on lotion
stay in bed
take asprin
take ibuprofen
take some medicine
use a heating pad

Making an Appointment

A. Read.

Receptionist: Hello, Dr. Walsh's office.

Patient: Hello, this is Mrs. Moreno.

Receptionist: Hello, Mrs. Moreno. How can I help you today?

Patient: My daughter is sick.

Receptionist: What's the problem?

Patient: She has a high fever and a sore throat.

Receptionist: Can you come in today at 2:00?

Patient: Yes, I can.

Receptionist: OK, Mrs. Moreno. See you at 2:00.

B. Complete the conversation with a partner.

Receptionist: Hello, Dr. _____'s office.

Patient: Hello, this is _____.

Receptionist: Hello, _____. How can I help you today?

Patient: _____.

Receptionist: What's the problem?

Patient: _____.

Receptionist: Can you come in today at _____?

Patient: _____.

Receptionist: OK, _____. See you at _____.

C. Act out the conversation.

Looking at Forms: Patient Information Form

A. Complete.

Culture Note
When you visit a doctor's office for the first time, you will have to fill out an information form or a medical information form.

Patient Information Form

Last Name _____ First Name _____ MI _____

Address _____

City _____ State _____

Zip Code _____

Home Telephone: _____ – _____ – _____

Work Telephone: _____ – _____ – _____

Employer _____

Insurance Company _____

Policy Number _____

Do you have any allergies to medication?   Yes   No

Explain _____

What is your problem today?

_____

_____

The Big Picture: In the Waiting Room

A. Listen.

B. Read and answer.

1. Who is getting a checkup?
2. Who has an allergy?
3. Who has a burn?
4. Who has a bad cough?
5. Who is working in the office?
6. Who is sick?
7. Who has a headache?
8. Who is getting a tetanus shot?
9. Who is a new patient?

tetanus shot

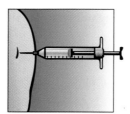

C. Read and circle.

1. Mrs. Jacob is the doctor. Yes (No)
2. Mrs. Lee has a headache. Yes No
3. Mr. Green has a cold. Yes No
4. Mrs. Rios has allergies. Yes No
5. Julia's finger hurts. Yes No
6. Mr. Patel has a bad back. Yes No
7. Mrs. Jackson is a new patient. Yes No
8. Miss Gonzalez's throat hurts. Yes No
9. Andy has a stomachache. Yes No

D. Complete.

1. Mrs. Lee has a _____ bad cough _____ .
2. Mr. Green needs a _____ .
3. Mr. Patel's _____ hurts.
4. Miss Gonzales has _____ .
5. She needs a _____ .
6. Andy needs a _____ .

> allergies
> checkup
> ✓bad cough
> head
> prescription
> tetanus shot

E. Read and circle.

1. Why is the waiting room busy? It's busy because . . .
   a. it's late.   b. the doctor is away.   (c.) many people are sick.
2. What is Mrs. Jackson going to fill out?
   a. a prescription   b. a patient information form   c. an application
3. What is Mrs. Lee doing?
   a. She's coughing.   b. She's talking to the nurse.   c. She's sneezing.
4. Mrs. Gonzales needs a prescription for _____ .
   a. allergies   b. asthma   c. a cold
5. How does Andy feel?
   a. sick   b. happy   c. scared

Reading: A Good Night's Sleep

A. Before You Read. Look at the chart. How many hours of sleep do you need?

Age	Hours of sleep per night
Adults	7–8 hours
Teenagers	8–9 hours
Children	10–12 hours

Is it difficult for you to fall asleep? Sometimes your body is tired, but your mind is still working. Here are some ideas for a good night's sleep:

1. Try to go to bed and get up at the same time every day.
2. Take a warm shower or bath before you go to bed.
3. Relax before you close your eyes. Watch TV, read a book, or listen to soft music.
4. Don't eat late at night.
5. Make your room quiet and comfortable. Turn off the light and close the curtains.
6. Drink a cup of warm milk before you go to bed. Don't drink coffee, tea, or alcohol. The caffeine in the drinks will keep you awake.

Everyone has trouble sleeping once in a while. If you have trouble sleeping for more than one month, see your doctor.

B. Read and answer.

1. Joseph is 16 years old. He goes to school, plays soccer after school, works from 6:00 to 9:00, and then does his homework until 12:00 A.M. He can't concentrate in school. What can he do?
2. Maribel has many family problems. When she goes to bed, she thinks about her children, her husband, and her sisters. She can't sleep. What can she do?
3. Mr. Andaba works from 3:00 to 11:00. When he gets home, he eats dinner. He goes to bed at 1:00, but he doesn't sleep well. What can he do?

Writing Our Stories:
My Lifestyle

A. Read.

I am 70 years old. I am a senior citizen. I think I am in good health. I am very active. I am retired, but I volunteer three days a week at the elementary school. I help the children read. I go to the park five days a week. I walk two miles every morning. I go to the doctor every year for a checkup, and I see my dentist twice a year. I am a healthy person.

B. Complete these sentences about your lifestyle.

1. I **am / am not** healthy.

2. I **always / sometimes / never** exercise.

3. I exercise _____ time(s) a week.

4. I get a checkup **every year / every other year**.

5. I visit the dentist **once a year / twice a year**.

6. I need to ☐ exercise more.
   ☐ **lose weight / gain weight**.
   ☐ visit the **doctor / dentist**.

Writing Note
Check the plural nouns in your story. Most plural nouns end in s: days, miles. Some plural nouns are irregular: **children**.

C. In your notebook, write about your health.

Practicing on Your Own

A. Describe the picture.

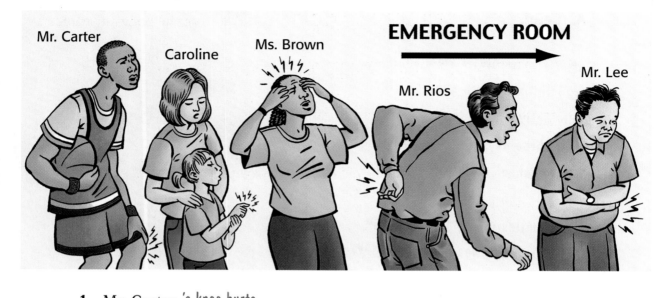

Mr. Carter   Caroline   Ms. Brown   **EMERGENCY ROOM**   Mr. Rios   Mr. Lee

1. Mr. Carter _'s knee hurts_ .

2. Caroline _____ .

3. Ms. Brown _____ .

4. Mr. Rios _____ .

5. Mr. Lee _____ .

B. Complete the sentences.

1. When I have a cold, I take _____ .

2. When I need a doctor, I call _____ .

3. When I have a headache, I _____ .

4. When my tooth hurts, I _____ .

5. When I have a sore throat, I _____ .

C. Read the directions. (Circle) *must* or *must not.*

> Take 2 capsules a day, 1 in the morning and 1 before bed.
> Do not take with milk or juice.
> Take with water.

1. The patient **must / must not** take this medicine three times a day.

2. The patient **must / must not** take this medicine with water.

Looking at Numbers: Reading a Thermometer

A. Read the temperature.

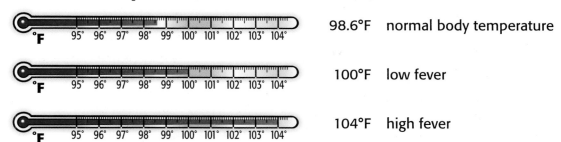

98.6°F   normal body temperature

100°F   low fever

104°F   high fever

B. Write the temperature. Circle *normal, low,* or *high fever.*

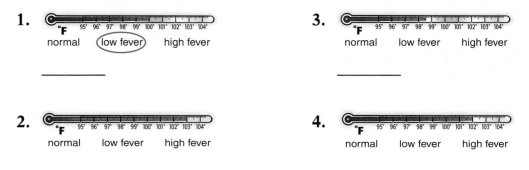

1.
normal   (low fever)   high fever

_____

2.
normal   low fever   high fever

_____

3.
normal   low fever   high fever

_____

4.
normal   low fever   high fever

_____

Grammar Summary

▶ **1. *Have / Has***

I **have** a fever.
You **have** a headache.
We **have** sore throats.
He **has** a stomachache.
She **has** asthma.
They **have** colds.

▶ **2. *My _____ hurt(s).***

My back **hurts.**
Your knee **hurts.**
Our feet **hurt.**
His arm **hurts.**
Her neck **hurts.**
Their stomachs **hurt.**

▶ **3. When I . . . , I . . .**

When I have a headache, **I** take aspirin.
When they have colds, **they** drink lots of liquids.

▶ **4. *Must / Must not***

An adult **must take** two teaspoons of this medicine.
A child **must not take** this medicine.

15 School

Dictionary: Classroom Activities, School Subjects

 A. Listen and repeat.

Classroom Activities

color

cut out pictures

jigsaw
do puzzles

draw

paint a picture

play an instrument

raise his hand

sing

sit in a circle

take a test

work in groups

work on the computer

School Subjects

art

foreign language

geography

handwriting

math

music

physical education

science

social studies

spelling

 Active Grammar: Present Tense

A. Listen and complete.

 1. Luisa _____ is playing _____ a game.

 2. Cesar _____ his hand.

 3. Yury _____ a picture.

 4. Irina and Marie _____ a story.

 5. Paul and Michelle _____ a video.

draw
✓play
raise
take
watch
work
read

6. Anita _____ a test.

7. Young Su _____ in a group.

B. Match the school subject with the picture.

1. Math

2. Art

3. Geography

4. Handwriting

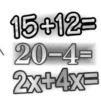

5. Music

6. Science

7. Physical Education

C. Pair practice. Ask and answer questions about school activities.

color	raise his hand
sing	talk to the teacher
draw a picture	work on the computer
play an instrument	write a report

What is he doing?

He's drawing a picture.

1.

2.

3.

4.

5.

6.

7.

8.

D. Describe your class. Circle Yes or No.

1. We watch videos.   Yes   No
2. We read books.   Yes   No
3. We read newspapers in English.   Yes   No
4. We sing songs in English.   Yes   No
5. We take tests.   Yes   No
6. We work on computers.   Yes   No
7. We draw pictures.   Yes   No
8. We _____.

Ordinal Numbers: Grades

A. Listen and repeat.

	1 first 1st	2 second 2nd	3 third 3rd	4 fourth 4th	5 fifth 5th
kindergarten					

6 sixth 6th	7 seventh 7th	8 eighth 8th	9 ninth 9th	10 tenth 10th	11 eleventh 11th	12 twelfth 12th

B. Complete.

Elementary School

1	2	3	4	5
first	_____	_____	_____	_____

Middle School

6	7	8
_____	_____	_____

High School

9	10	11	12
_____	_____	_____	_____

C. Pronunciation: Ordinal numbers. Listen and repeat.

a. 1   1st   e. 5   5th   i. 9   9th

b. 2   2nd   f. 6   6th   j. 10 10th

c. 3   3rd   g. 7   7th   k. 11 11th

d. 4   4th   h. 8   8th   l. 12 12th

D. Listen and (circle.)

a. ③ 3rd   d. 10 10th   g. 8   8th

b. 12 12th   e. 7   7th   h. 6   6th

c. 4   4th   f. 11 11th   i. 9   9th

E. Listen and (circle.)

1. elementary   (middle)   high school

2. elementary   middle   high school

3. elementary   middle   high school

4. elementary   middle   high school

5. elementary   middle   high school

6. elementary   middle   high school

F. Complete.

1. My _____daughter_____ is in the _____third_____
   grade in _____elementary_____ school.

2. My _____ is in the _____
   grade in _____ school.

3. My _____ is in the _____
   grade in _____ school.

| brother |
| sister |
| son |
| daughter |
| grandson |
| granddaughter |
| friend |

Report Card

 A. Listen and complete.

doesn't follow	doesn't pay	doesn't get along
doesn't do	doesn't raise	

☑ **Her behavior needs improvement.**

1. Paula _____ her hand to answer questions.

2. She _____ attention.

3. She _____ with her classmates.

4. She _____ her homework.

5. She _____ directions.

B. Complete with a partner.

Present Tense
He follows directions.
He works in a group.

☑ **Excellent behavior**

1. Victor _____raises_____ his hand to answer questions.

2. He always _____ his homework.

3. He _____ very well with his classmates.

4. He _____ to the teacher.

C. Read the report card.

Pupil	Rani Singh				School	Emerson School			
Teacher	Mrs. Lawson				Principal	Mr. Hobbie			

Pupil Progress Report   Grade 4

A = Excellent   B = Very Good   C = Satisfactory   D = Poor   F = Not Passing

Subjects	1	2	3	4	Social Skills	1	2	3	4
Math	A	A	A		Follows school rules	B	A	B	
Art	A	B	B		Pays attention to teacher	A	B	A	
Handwriting	C	B	A		Works and plays well with others	C	B	A	
Music	B	B	B		**Work**				
Physical Education	C	B	B		Takes care of books	B	B	B	
Spelling	B	A	A		Follows directions	A	B	A	
Social Studies	C	B	C		Does homework well and on time	B	B	A	
Science	A	A	A		Asks for help	C	C	B	

D. Answer.

1. What are two of Rani's best subjects?
2. What subject is more difficult for Rani?
3. Does Rani work and play well with others?
4. Is Rani a good student? Why or why not?

Culture Note

Most public schools give report cards to the students four times a year. The parents must sign the report card and return it to school.

Working Together

A. Complete the information about your child's education or the education of a child you know well. Compare with a group of three or four classmates.

1. The name of my _____'s school is _____.

2. My _____ is in _____ grade.

3. The school is in _____.

city

4. The school is on _____.

street

5. The teacher is _____.

6. The principal is _____.

B. Complete about the child in Exercise A.

1. _____ **likes / doesn't like** the school.

name of the child

2. _____ **likes / doesn't like** the teacher.

name of the child

3. I **like / don't like** the teacher.

4. _____ **is / isn't** learning to play an instrument.

He/She

5. _____ **is / isn't** learning how to use a computer.

He/She

6. _____ **is / isn't** studying science.

He/She

7. _____ **is / isn't** learning another language.

He/She

8. _____ **is / isn't** in a club at the school.

He/She

9. _____

Helping A Child Succeed in School

A. Read.

Read to her.

Help her with her homework.

Give her a quiet place to study.

B. Read this list of ways to help a child in school.

1. Take her to the library.
2. Talk with her teacher regularly.
3. Go on field trips with her class.
4. Encourage her to play a musical instrument.
5. Encourage her to play a sport or to join a school club.

C. In your notebook, write two more ways to help a child in school.

The Big Picture: In the Classroom

A. Listen.

B. Listen again and label the people.

Ricky	Marta	Gloria	Nancy	Mr. Washington
Vicky	Ernest	Mei	Steve	

C. Read and circle.

1. Yes   (No)   This is a sixth-grade class.

2. Yes   No   Mr. Washington is using the computers.

3. Yes   No   Ernest is drawing a map.

4. Yes   No   Ricky is raising his hand.

5. Yes   No   Mei is painting a picture.

6. Yes   No   Steve is reading alone.

7. Yes   No   Steve likes to work in groups.

8. Yes   No   All of the students are working in groups.

D. Complete. Some of the sentences are negative.

do	help	raise	work
draw	read	sit	

1. The students _____are doing_____ final projects.

2. Mr. Washington _____ the students.

3. Most of the students _____ in groups.

4. Students _____ on computers.

5. Ernest and Nancy _____ a map.

6. Marta has a question, so she _____ her hand.

7. Steve _____ with other students. He's working alone.

8. Gloria and Mei _____ on the computer, but Ricky and Vicky are.

E. Pair practice. Ask and answer questions about your English class.

Do you take tests in your class?

Do you work in groups in your class?

Yes, I do.

No, I don't.

Present Tense
Do you . . . ?
Yes, I do.
No, I don't.

practice pronunciation

raise your hand

study U.S. geography

practice handwriting

draw pictures

work on computers

Reading: School Uniforms—Yes or No?

A. Before You Read.

1. Do your children or children you know wear uniforms?

2. What kinds of schools require school uniforms?

Culture Note

State and local taxes pay for public school education. Parents must pay for private school and religious school education.

① In the past, only students in U.S. private and religious schools wore uniforms to school. Today, many states are changing. Many public schools require students to wear uniforms to school. Some people like uniforms, but others don't.

There are many reasons to have school uniforms. One reason is to decrease theft. In some schools, people steal expensive clothing. Students do not think about their expensive sneakers or designer jackets when they wear uniforms. A second reason is discipline. Principals and teachers think students pay better attention when they wear uniforms. A third reason is safety. A security guard can easily see a stranger in the school. Another reason is for school spirit. When all the students are wearing uniforms, the students feel part of a group. Finally, for students who don't have much money, uniforms are cheap.

Many students don't like school uniforms. They want to decide what to wear. What do you think? Do you think school uniforms are a good idea?

B. Answer. Underline the answers in the reading.

1. In the past, which students wore uniforms?

2. Does everyone like school uniforms?

3. Why do school uniforms help decrease theft?

4. Why do principals and teachers like school uniforms?

5. Are uniforms more expensive than regular clothes?

C. List the five reasons why many schools have uniforms.

Writing Our Stories:
An Absence Note

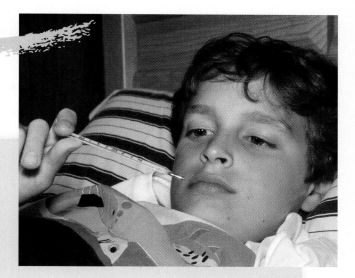

A. Read.

May 1, 2003

Dear Mrs. Woods,
    Please excuse Billy's absence from school on Monday and Tuesday. He could not come to school because he had a fever and cold. Please give him the homework.

Sincerely,
Mrs. Collins

B. Write an absence note.

_____
Date

Dear _____ ,
    Name of teacher

    Please excuse _____

_____. _____ could not come to

school because _____ .

Please _____ .

Sincerely,

_____

Writing Note

Circle the commas in this letter. Where do you use a comma?

 Practicing on Your Own

Yes, I do.	No, I don't.
Yes, she does.	No, she doesn't.
Yes, he does.	No, he doesn't.
Yes, we do.	No, we don't.
Yes, they do.	No, they don't.

A. Write the answers about your class and your teacher.

1. Do you always do your homework? _____

2. Does your teacher give homework every day? _____

3. Do you and your classmates get along? _____

4. Do you try to speak English in every class? _____

5. Do you play games in class? _____

6. Do your classmates speak your native language? _____

7. Does your teacher help you after class? _____

8. Does your teacher write on the blackboard? _____

B. Read and complete.

Jason is a poor student. His behavior needs improvement.

Patty is a good student. Her behavior is excellent.

doesn't do	doesn't pay	doesn't get along
does	pays	gets along
	follows	doesn't follow

1. Jason ___doesn't___ ___pay___ attention in class.

2. Patty _____ her homework every day.

3. Patty _____ the teacher's directions.

4. Jason _____ _____ his homework.

5. Patty _____ _____ well with the other students.

6. Jason _____ _____ _____ with the other students.

> **I raise my hand in class.**
> **I try to talk and answer questions.**
> **It's OK if I make a mistake.**

☐ I like this idea.
☐ I don't like this idea.
☐ I'm going to try this idea.

Grammar Summary

▶ **1. Present tense**	
He **pays** attention.	She **doesn't pay** attention.
He **raises** his hand.	She **doesn't raise** her hand.
▶ **2. Present-tense *yes/no* questions**	
Do you **have** computers?	Yes, I **do.**
Do you **take** tests?	No, I **don't.**
▶ **3. Present continuous**	
He **is drawing** a picture.	
She **is working** on a computer.	
They **are sitting** in a circle.	

Audio Script

Unit 1: Hello

Page 7

F. Look at Exercise E again. Circle the sentence you hear.

1. He is from Mexico.
2. She's from Vietnam.
3. I'm from Russia.
4. He's from China.
5. I am from Haiti.
6. She is from Peru.
7. He's from Cuba.
8. She's from Egypt.

Page 8

D. Listen and circle.

a. 1 **b.** 8 **c.** 10 **d.** 0 **e.** 7 **f.** 14 **g.** 20 **h.** 6 **i.** 13 **j.** 2 **k.** 12 **l.** 19

Page 9

B. Listen and write.

a. 555-3231 **b.** 555-3692 **c.** 555-7548 **d.** 555-3080
e. 201-555-4413 **f.** 800-555-4242 **g.** 619-555-7042 **h.** 813-555-1624

Page 11

The Big Picture: My Classmates

A. Listen.

Hi. My name is Tomas. I'm a student in English 1. I'm in class now. Here are four students in my class. This is Hiro. He's from Japan. This is Erica. She's from Mexico. This is Marie. She's from Haiti. This is Jenny. She's from Hong Kong. And this is me. I'm from Peru.

D. Listen. Write the number next to the answer.

1. What's your name?
2. Where are you from?
3. What's his name?
4. Where is he from?
5. What's her name?
6. Where is she from?

Unit 2: The Classroom

Page 20

A. Listen. Number the conversations.

Conversation 1
A: Is this your book?
B: Yes, it is. Thank you.

Conversation 2
A: Is this your eraser?
B: Yes, it is. Thank you.

Conversation 3
A: Is this your pencil?
B: No, it isn't.

B. Listen and complete.

1. Is this your dictionary?
   Yes, it is. Thank you.
2. Is this your pen?
   Yes, it is. Thank you.
3. Is this your pencil sharpener?
   No, it isn't.
4. Is this your paper?
   Yes, it is. Thank you.
5. Is this your notebook?
   No, it isn't.

Page 22

A. Pronunciation: Plural nouns. Listen and circle.

1. a pencil
2. students
3. teachers
4. men
5. a map
6. a dictionary
7. an eraser
8. notebooks
9. classrooms
10. a woman

Page 23

B. Listen and circle.

a. 17   b. 7   c. 16   d. 8   e. 27   f. 26   g. 33   h. 12   i. 45   j. 56   k. 76   l. 89

Page 24

A. Listen.

There is a dictionary on the desk.
There's a piece of paper on the desk.
There are two pens on the desk.
There are three pencils on the desk.

There are five books on the desk.
There's an eraser on the desk.
There's a notebook on the desk.

Page 26

The Big Picture: The Classroom

B. Listen.

I am a student in English 1. My classroom is on the second floor in Room 204. There are ten students in my class. There are four men and six women. We are from many different countries. There are five students from Mexico. There are two students from Vietnam. There is one student from El Salvador, one from India, and one from the Philippines.

Our room is small. There is a big table in the front for the teacher. There are twelve desks for the students. There is a chalkboard on the wall. There are two maps on the wall, one of the United States and one of the world.

Our teacher is Mr. Wilson. We like our teacher, and we like our class.

Page 27

C. Listen and circle.

1. The classroom is in Room 208.
2. There are twelve students in this class.
3. There are ten men in this class.
4. There are six women in this class.
5. There are four children in this class.
6. There are five students from India.
7. There is one student from El Salvador.
8. The room is small.
9. There are two maps on the wall.
10. We like our class.

Unit 3: The Family

Page 33

B. Family photographs. Listen to the conversations. Number the photographs.

Conversation 1
A: This is my daughter, Lana, and her little boy. His name is Michael, and he's four years old. He's our first grandchild.
B: How old is Lana?
A: She's 35.

Conversation 2
A: This is my son, Brian. He's three. And this is our daughter, Erica.
B: How old is Erica?
A: She's six.
B: That's a beautiful picture.

Conversation 3
A: This is my daughter, Silvia. She's 25. And this is her husband, Carlos. He's 28. They live in Florida.
B: Do they have any children?
A: No, they don't.

Page 36

C. Listen. Write the date.

1. January 4, 2003
2. February 11, 1982
3. April 17, 1976
4. July 25, 1990
5. August 18, 2005
6. September 7, 1964
7. November 30, 1999
8. December 25, 2000

Page 40

The Big Picture: A Family Photo

B. Listen. Write these names on the picture.

A: I have the pictures from the party last week.

B: Oh, yes, your mom's birthday party. Let me see.

A: Here's a picture of everyone.

B: Oh, That's you and Steve. And your two little girls. Which one is Emily, and which one is Kim?

A: Emily is five. She has long hair. And Kim is six. She has short hair.

B: Now, that's your mom and dad. Right? In the middle?

A: Yes. That's mom. It's her birthday. She's 55 years old. And that's dad, next to her.

B: Oh, your dad has a moustache!

A: Yes. He has a moustache. At one time, he had curly hair, but now he's bald.

B: Who's this?

A: These are my sisters. I have two sisters. This is my sister Joanne. She's 21. And next to her, that's my sister Mary. She's 23.

B: Joanne and Mary look a lot alike.

A: I know. They're tall and they both have dark, curly hair. But Joanne is a little heavy, and Mary is very thin.

B: Are your sisters married?

A: No, I'm the only one who is married.

B: And who's this?

A: That's my brother, Andy.

B: Oh, you have a brother?

A: Yes, I have a brother. Andy is the baby of the family. He's 18.

B: He looks like your dad.

A: Hmm. You're right.

B: That's a great picture.

Page 41

F. Pronunciation. Listen and repeat.

Statements	Questions
He is tall.	Is he tall?
She is short.	Is she short?
It is curly.	Is it curly?

Listen and complete.

1. She is old.
2. Is he young?
3. Is it heavy?
4. It is tall.

5. She is thin.
6. Is he tall?
7. Is she short?
8. He is heavy.

Unit 4: Moving Day

Page 52

C. Listen. Write the addresses.

1 **a.** 73 North Avenue

2 **b.** 66 Maple Street

3 **c.** 143 Central Avenue

4 **d.** 861 Park Avenue

5 **e.** 9924 First Street

6 **f.** 3285 Main Street

Page 54

The Big Picture: A Dorm Room

B. Listen to this conversation between Kathy and her father.

F: Your dorm room is very small, Kathy.

K: I know. It is small. But everything is in my room now.

F: Tell me about your room. Where did you put everything?

K: Well, the bed is on the right. My pillow is under the window. The night table is at the end of my bed, and the TV is on the table.

F: Where's the dresser?

K: The dresser is on the left. I put the stereo on the dresser, and my CDs are next to the stereo.

F: Where's your desk?

K: It's next to my dresser. I put the small bookcase on my desk. The computer is on the desk, and the printer is next to the computer.

F: Where are your clothes?

K: Most of my clothes are in the closet.

F: And where's your telephone?

K: It's under the bed!

Unit 5: I'm Busy

Page 61

C. Circle the form you hear.

1. He's walking.
2. She is cleaning.
3. I am making lunch.
4. You're driving.
5. They're watching TV.
6. We are studying.

Page 66

The Big Picture: Where is everybody?

A. Listen to the conversation between Tommy and his mother.

Tommy: Hello.

Mom: Hi, Tommy. This is Mommy.

Tommy: Hi, Mommy. Are you at work?

Mom: Yes, I'm a little late. What are you doing? Are you doing your homework?

Tommy: No, I'm not. I'm watching TV.

Mom: Where's Brian? Is he doing his homework?

Tommy: Brian's in the living room. He's playing video games.

Mom: And Katie? Where's Katie?

Tommy: She's in her bedroom.

Mom: Good! Is she doing her homework?

Tommy: No, Mom. She's talking on the telephone to her boyfriend.

Mom: Where's Daddy? Is he cooking dinner?

Tommy: Daddy's in the living room. He's sleeping.

Mom: I'm coming home right now.

Page 67

D. Listen and answer.

1. Is Mom at home?
2. Is she talking to Tommy?
3. Is Tommy doing his homework?
4. Is Brian doing his homework?
5. Is Brian playing video games?
7. Is Dad cooking dinner?
6. Is Katie doing her homework?

Unit 6: My City

Page 76

B. Listen and complete with an adjective.

1. Miles City, Montana, is a small city.
2. The movies in New York City are expensive.
3. Downtown Chicago is busy.
4. The weather in Phoenix, Arizona, is hot and dry.
5. The people in Atlanta, Georgia, are friendly.
6. The streets in San Francisco, California, are clean.
7. The traffic in Boston, Massachusetts, is heavy.
8. New Orleans, Louisiana, is an interesting city.

Page 79

A. Listen and complete.

Conversation 1

A: What city do you want to visit?

Janet: I want to visit San Diego.

A: Why do you want to visit San Diego?

Janet: I want to visit San Diego because it is a beautiful city.

Conversation 2
A: What city do you want to visit?
Steven: I want to visit New York City.
A: Why do you want to visit New York City?
Steven: I want to visit New York because it's very exciting.

Conversation 3
A: What city do you want to visit?
Caroline: We want to visit Orlando.
A: Why do you want to visit Orlando?
Caroline: We want to visit Orlando because it's fun.

Page 80

A. Listen.
1. The population of Miami, Florida, is 369,253.
2. The population of Atlanta, Georgia, is 401,766.
3. The population of Las Vegas, Nevada, is 418, 658.
4. The population of Washington, D.C., is 519,000.
5. The population of Detroit, Michigan, is 965,084.
6. The population of San Antonio, Texas, is 1,147,213.
7. The population of Philadelphia, Pennsylvania, is 1,417,601.
8. The population of Houston, Texas, is 1,845,967.
9. The population of Los Angeles, California, is 3,633,591.
10. The population of New York, New York, is 7,428,162.

Page 80

B. Listen and write the populations.
1. The population of Seattle, Washington, is 563,374.
2. The population of Phoenix, Arizona, is 1,211,466.
3. The population of San Francisco, California, is 745,774.
4. The population of Boston, Massachusetts, is 555,249.
5. The population of Chicago, Illinois, is 2,799, 050.
6. The population of Fresno, California, is 404,141.
7. The population of Honolulu, Hawaii, is 395,327.
8. The population of Dallas, Texas, is 1,075,894.

Page 84

The Big Picture: Chicago, Illinois

Chicago, Illinois, is one of the largest cities in the U.S. It's in the Midwest of the country next to beautiful Lake Michigan. The summers are hot, and the winters are cold, so visit Chicago in the spring or in the fall.

There are many interesting places to visit. Many places are in busy downtown Chicago. If you like art, go to the Art Institute of Chicago. There are many famous paintings there. But, if you like something different, go to one of Chicago's blues clubs. You'll see Chicago's great blues musicians. Maybe you'll want to dance.

If you like sports, Chicago is for you. It's a great sports town. There are seven professional teams in Chicago. Wrigley Field, a baseball park, is the oldest baseball park in the United States. It's home to the Chicago Cubs baseball team.

For children, there are also many places to visit. The Brookfield Zoo is a fun place for children. Children will also like the Sears Tower office building. It is one of the tallest buildings in the world. It has 110 floors. You can take an elevator to the top and see all of Chicago.

Do you watch TV talk shows? Then you know Oprah Winfrey. Her talk show is very popular. Millions of people watch her TV show every afternoon. If you go to Chicago, maybe you can watch the Oprah show live!

So, when do you want to visit Chicago? Chicago is waiting for you.

Unit 7: Downtown

Page 92

A. Listen and complete the map.

1. **A:** Where's the bakery?
   B: It's on Main Street, next to the park.
2. **A:** Where's the supermarket?
   B: It's across from the post office.
3. **A:** Where's the shoe store?
   B: It's on Main Street, across from the drugstore.
4. **A:** Where's the bookstore?
   B: It's next to the shoe store.
5. **A:** Where's the library?
   B: It's on Maple Avenue. It's behind the post office.
6. **A:** Where's the bank?
   B: It's on the corner of Main Street and First Street.
7. **A:** Where's the coffee shop?
   B: It's next to the post office.
8. **A:** Where's the laundromat?
   B: It's on the corner of Second Street and Maple Avenue.

Page 95

B. Listen and write the locations on the map.

1. **A:** Where's City Hall?
   B: Walk two blocks to Broad Street.
   Turn left. City Hall is on your right.
2. **A:** Where's the library?
   B: Walk three blocks to the first traffic light.
   Turn left. The library is two blocks up on your right.
3. **A:** Where's the hospital?
   B: Walk three blocks to the first traffic light.
   Turn right. The hospital is on your left.
4. **A:** Where's the aquarium?
   B: Walk four blocks to the second traffic light. That's Clark Street.
   Turn right. The aquarium is on your left.

Page 98

The Big Picture: Downtown

A. Listen.

It's a busy afternoon downtown. People are busy, and the stores are busy, too. Oh, look! There's an accident at the intersection of Smith Street and North Main Street. Mr. Thomas works at the bakery, and he drives the delivery truck. He's talking to the other driver. Over in the park, Elena is watching the children. The children are playing on swings. They're having a good time. There's a coffee shop on North Main Street. There are two tables in front of the coffee shop. Joseph is sitting at a table. He's reading the newspaper and drinking a cup of coffee. Jane is sitting at the other table. She's reading a good book. Mark is the waiter. He's bringing Jane some ice cream. Uh, oh. Mrs. Lee is running to her car. Officer Ortiz is standing next to her car. He's writing her a ticket. Oh, how wonderful! Michael and Luisa are in front of City Hall. I think they're getting married today.

B. Listen and circle.

1. Who is watching the children?
2. Who is getting married?
3. Who is standing at the corner of Smith Street and North Main Street?
4. Who is running?
5. Who is working at the coffee shop?
6. Who is reading a book?
7. Who is drinking a cup of coffee?
8. Who is writing a ticket?

Unit 8: Money

Page 105

C. Listen and write the amount.

a. two cents
b. ten cents
c. seventeen cents

d. twenty-five cents
e. thirty-eight cents
f. forty-nine cents

g. fifty cents
h. sixty-nine cents
i. ninety-eight cents

Page 106

B. Listen and write the amount.

a. a dollar
b. a dollar twenty-five
c. two dollars and fifty cents
d. three seventy-five
e. fifteen dollars and eight cents

f. seventy-nine twenty-five
g. one hundred fifty-seven dollars and sixty-two cents
h. two hundred thirty dollars and ninety-nine cents
i. four hundred fifty-seven dollars and twenty-four cents

C. Listen and repeat.

13, 14, 15, 16, 17, 18, 19, 20
30, 40, 50, 60, 70, 80, 90, 100

Circle.

a. 13 b. 40 c. 15 d. 60 e. 70 f. 18 g. 19 h. $13.50 i. $15.99
j. $19.99 k. $14.14 l. $17.20 m. $16.16 n. $18.75

Page 114

The Big Picture: The Electronics Store

B. Listen.

Electronics City is having a July 4th sale, and all their electronic equipment is on sale. A lot of customers are in the store and the salespeople are busy.

Marta is standing in front of the big-screen TVs. She watches TV a lot. On Saturday and Sunday she watches sports, like soccer, baseball, and tennis. She wants a big-screen to enjoy the games. Tammy and Sean are expecting their first baby soon. They are looking at video cameras. They want to take lots of pictures of the baby for their parents. George is looking at the DVDs. He likes movies, and the DVDs are on sale for $12.99 each or three for $30.00. He's going to buy three. Tamara is Russian, and she's studying English. She's buying an English-Russian electronic dictionary to help her with vocabulary. Mr. and Mrs. Jackson want to buy their first computer. They want to e-mail their children and their grandchildren. They don't know anything about computers. Their grandson is helping them buy the right computer. Then he is going to show them how to use it.

Page 115

E. Listen to each conversation. Write the item and the price.

Conversation 1
A: Is this a Russian-English dictionary?
B: Yes, it is.
A: How much is it?
B: It's $39.99.
A: I'll take it.

Conversation 2
A: What size is this TV?
B: It's a 50".
A: Is it on sale?
B: Yes. It's usually $1,699. But it's on sale today for $1,549.

Conversation 3
A: How much is this computer?
B: It's $1,999.
A: We need an easy-to-use computer. We just need it for e-mail. What else do you have?
B: This is our basic model. It's very easy to use. It's only $599.

Conversation 4

A: This is a nice video camera. Is it easy to use?
B: Yes, it's very easy to use. And the pictures are great.
A: Can I connect it to my TV?
B: You can connect it to your TV or your computer.
A: How long is the warranty?
B: It's one year.
A: How much is it?
B: It's on sale for $799. And there's a $100 rebate.
A: What's a rebate?
B: Send this card and a copy of your receipt to the manufacturer. They will send you $100.

Unit 9: Working at the Mall

Page 124

C. Listen and show the times on the clocks.
a. four o'clock
b. six thirty
c. eight fifteen
d. ten fifty-five

Page 127

B. Listen and complete.

Picture 1
A: Where do you work?
B: I work at Family Pharmacy.
A: What do you do?
B: I'm a pharmacist. I fill prescriptions and talk to customers.
A: Do you work full time or part time?
B: Full time.
A: What's your schedule?
B: I work from Monday to Friday, from 12:00 to 8:00.
A: Do you like your job?
B: Yes, I do.

Picture 2
A: Where do you work?
B: I work at the Flower Basket.
A: What do you do?
B: I'm a florist. I sell flowers and plants.
A: Do you work full time or part time?
B: I work part time.
A: What's your schedule?
B: I work from Wednesday to Saturday, from 9:00 to 2:00.
A: Do you like your job?
B: Yes, I do.

Page 130

The Big Picture: The CD Den

A. Listen.

My name is Eric. I'm the manager of the CD Den in the Summit Mall. We sell CDs and tapes of all kinds of music—rock, pop, jazz, classical. We have the music you want. In our store, there is always music playing.

The CD Den is open seven days a week from 10 A.M. to 9 P.M. I work full time, about 50 hours a week. My assistant manager, Mei-Lin, also works full time. All the other employees are part time. We have 10 part-time workers. Most of them are high school and college students. They work about 15 to 20 hours a week, after school and on the weekends. Those are our busiest times. On the weekends, we have a security guard, too. She is young, and she doesn't wear a uniform. She looks like a customer. She walks around the store and watches people.

Page 131

D. Listen. Write the day and times.

1. **Eric:** James, can you work Monday?
   James: What time Monday?
   Eric: From 5:00 to 9:00.
   James: Sure. 5:00 to 9:00. That's OK.
2. **Eric:** Gloria, I need someone Tuesday, from 3:00 to 7:00. Can you work then?
   Gloria: Tuesday. 3:00 to 7:00. No problem. I can work.
3. **Eric:** Makiko, I need another person Saturday. Can you work this Saturday from 10:00 to 5:00?
   Makiko: Yes, I can work Saturday.
4. **Eric:** Andre, can you work Sunday from 10:00 to 6:00?
   Andre: I can't start at 10:00. I can start at 12:00.
   Eric: OK. Sunday, from 12:00 to 6:00. That's good.
5. **Eric:** Lucy, can you work Friday this week? I need you from 5:00 to 10:00.
   Lucy: That's good for me. I can work Friday.

Unit 10: Clothing and Weather

Page 139

D. Listen. What is Amy wearing? Write the letter of the correct picture.

1. She's wearing a blue dress.
2. She's wearing beige shorts.
3. She's wearing black pants.
4. She's wearing a big white belt.
5. She's wearing a green shirt.
6. She's wearing a white blouse.
7. She's wearing sneakers.
8. She's wearing a green jacket.
9. She's wearing white sandals.
10. She's carrying a white sweater.

Page 143

B. Listen to the weather. Find the city and write the temperature on the map.

Look at the map of the United States.
Find Boston. It's cold in Boston today. It's snowing. The temperature is 20 degrees.
Find New York. It's cloudy and cold in New York today. The temperature is 35 degrees.
Find Miami. It's sunny and hot in Miami. The temperature is 80 degrees.
Find Houston. It's sunny and warm in Houston today. The temperature is 70 degrees.
Find San Diego. The weather is beautiful in San Diego all year. It's sunny and 75 degrees.
Find San Francisco. It's raining today in San Francisco. It's cool. The temperature is 55 degrees.
Find Seattle. It's raining in Seattle, too. It's 50 degrees in Seattle. You will need your umbrella and raincoat.
Find Denver. It's snowing in Denver today. It's 30 degrees in Denver.
Find Chicago. It's cloudy and cold in Chicago today. It's very windy. The temperature is 25 degrees.

Page 146

The Big Picture: The Clothing Store.

A. Listen. Circle the clothes Monica is going to buy.

Monica is from Cuba. Cuba is an island in the Caribbean, and it's hot there all year. Now Monica is living in Boston. Monica came to the United States in May. She liked the weather in Boston in May, June, July, and August. It was sunny and hot. September was warm, and Monica was comfortable. But now it is December. Monica can't believe the weather! It's very cold. It's 30 degrees. Her friends tell her, "This isn't cold yet! In January, it's going to be colder. And it's going to snow soon." Monica is at the clothing store with her sister. She needs warm clothes. She needs a coat. She needs a hat and gloves. She is also going to buy a sweater. Monica is standing in front of the mirror. She's trying on coats. She isn't comfortable. She's saying, "This coat feels so heavy."

Unit 11: Food

Page 154

B. Listen. What does he eat?

Hi, my name is Mike. I eat three meals a day. In the morning, I am always in a hurry, so I eat a small breakfast at 7:15. I eat a bagel and a piece of fruit. I always have a cup of coffee. Then I go to work. I eat lunch at 1:00. I have an hour for lunch. I like to have a sandwich, french fries, and a soda. Sometimes I buy some cookies for dessert. I eat dinner at home at 7:00. I like to cook, so I have a nice dinner. I have chicken, green beans, and a potato. I drink water. I don't have any dessert.

Page 157

B. What'll you have? Listen and write the order.

Waiter: May I take your order?

Woman: Yes, I'll have a large green salad. What's the soup of the day?

Waiter: Black bean.

Woman: I'll have the soup, too.

Waiter: Anything to drink?

Woman: Just water, please.

Waiter: And you, sir, what'll you have?

Man: I'll have a cheeseburger.

Waiter: How do you want your cheeseburger cooked?

Man: Medium, please.

Waiter: Anything to drink?

Man: I'll have iced tea.

Page 158

A. Pronunciation. Listen and complete. Then listen and repeat.

1. **I'll have** a salad.
2. **She'll have** a cup of tea.
3. **He'll have** a hamburger.
4. **He'll have** a small soda.
5. **I'll have** a glass of juice.
6. **She'll have** pancakes.
7. **We'll have** a cheese pizza.
8. **They'll have** pasta.

Page 162

The Big Picture: At Mario's Italian Restaurant

A. Listen.

It's Friday night at Mario's Italian Restaurant. Troy and Emma always eat at Mario's on Friday nights. They're sitting at their favorite table, near the window. Faye is the waitress. She always works on Friday nights, so Troy and Emma always sit at her table. Faye is friendly, so Troy and Emma give her a good tip. Right now, she is taking Troy's and Emma's orders. Troy is ordering a salad and chicken. Emma is ordering a salad and pasta. Bob and Ann are at the restaurant with their children, Lori and Matthew. Bob and Ann like to go out to eat on Fridays because they're always tired on Friday nights after a busy week. They're eating a large cheese-and-pepperoni pizza. They're all drinking soda.

Unit 12: Finding an Apartment

Page 170

A. Listen and circle.

1. Is there a kitchen in the house?
2. Are there three bedrooms in the house?
3. Are there many windows?
4. Is there only one bathroom?
5. Is there a garage?
6. Is there a closet near the door?
7. Is there a washer/dryer in the house?

C. Listen and write.

1. The **paint** is peeling.
2. The **ceiling** is leaking.
3. A **window** is stuck.
4. The **heat** is off.
5. The **neighbors** are noisy.
6. The **electricity** is off.
7. There is a **mouse** in the apartment.

Page 173

A. Listen. Match the conversation and the problem. Then circle the time.

Conversation 1

A: Hello, Mr. Williams. This is Mrs. Lopez in Apt. 3C.

B: Hello, Mrs. Lopez.

A: Could you come right away? It's 100 degrees in here. My air conditioner isn't working.

B: Your air conditioner isn't working?

A: That's right.

B: I'll be there right away.

Conversation 2

A: Hello, Mr. Williams. This is Miss DeVico in Apt. 5F.

B: Hello, Miss DeVico.

A: Aghh! Please come right away! There's a mouse in my kitchen!

B: A mouse in the kitchen?

A: Yes! Aghhh! Hurry up!

B: I'm coming right now.

Conversation 3

A: Hello, Mr. Williams. This is Mr. Martins in Apt. 14D.

B: Hello, Mr. Martins.

A: The kitchen faucet has a small leak. Can you come look at it?

B: The faucet is leaking? Mr. Martins, I'm very busy today.

A: When can you come fix it?

B: I'll be there tomorrow.

Conversation 4

A: Hello, Mr. Williams. This is Mrs. Walker in 12B.

B: Hello, Mrs. Walker. How are you today?

A: I'm very upset. I'm trying to cook dinner, and the stove isn't working.

B: The stove isn't working?

A: That's right. When can you come fix it?

B: I'm a little busy right now, but I'll be there later.

Conversation 5

A: Hello, Mr. Williams. This is Mr. Young in 24A.

B: Hello, Mr Young.

A: Mr. Williams, I think there's a leak in my ceiling. There's water on the floor.

B: Is it a big leak?

A: I don't think so. There's only a little water on the floor.

B: OK, I'll be there later this afternoon.

Conversation 6

A: Hi, Mr. Williams. This is Miss Dorisme in 10D.

B: Hello, Miss Dorisme. How are you?

A: Not well. I can't lock my door. I think the lock is broken.

B: I'll be there right away.

Page 176

The Big Picture: My Neighborhood

A. Listen.

Hi, I'm Ana Lee. This is my apartment and my neighborhood. I live in a one-bedroom apartment on the third floor. There's no elevator, so I walk up and down the stairs. I have a small bedroom, but it's very sunny. I have a small bathroom, a living room, and a kitchen. I would like to have a pet, but I can't have any pets in my building.

I like my neighborhood. It's quiet, safe, and convenient. I'm near everything. The park is across the street, so I walk in the park every morning. I shop at the market, and I can pay my phone bill at the telephone company. Best of all, I can walk to work because I teach at the elementary school down the street. Finally, I have great neighbors. Mr. and Mrs. Robinson live next door, and my friend Kevin lives in the apartment on the other side. My neighbors are quiet, and they're very friendly.

Unit 13: Applying for a Job

Page 185

A. Listen to each person talk about his or her job experience. Write the number of the speaker under each picture.

1. I work in a large hotel. I can use a computer and register guests. I talk to people every day.
2. I work in the hotel kitchen. I can cook Mexican food and Italian food.

3. I work in the basement. I can operate a large washing machine and dryer. I can wash and fold towels and sheets.
4. I have a lot of experience. I can repair an air conditioner, a fan, or your lights. I work in many different rooms in the hotel.

Page 186

A. Listen and complete.

1. In my country, Colombia, I was a Spanish teacher in a high school. Now I am a van driver at a hotel. I am studying for my teaching certificate. I want to teach Spanish to high school students.
2. In my country, Poland, I was a manager in a four-star hotel. Now I am a desk clerk in a small hotel. I can make reservations and use a computer. I am preparing for a management job.
3. In my country, Brazil, I was a dance teacher. Now I am a waitress in a hotel. I am studying English and dance at a community college. I can do the samba, salsa, and teach many dances. I want to get a degree.

Page 186

B. Pronunciation: *Was*. Listen and repeat.

1. I am a cook.	I was a cook.
2. I am a mechanic.	I was a mechanic.
3. He is a landscaper.	He was a landscaper.
4. She is a housewife.	She was a housewife.
5. He is a teacher.	He was a teacher.
6. She is a manager.	She was a manager.
7. I am a plumber.	I was a plumber.
8. He is a security guard.	He was a security guard.

Page 187

C. Listen and circle *Now* or *Past*.

1. I was an electrician in my country.
2. I am a desk clerk at a small motel.
3. I was the head cook at a Polish restaurant.
4. I was a housewife and stayed home with my children.
5. I am a van driver, and I drive passengers to the airport.
6. I am a babysitter for a family.
7. I was a security guard in a bank.
8. I am a waitress in a Colombian restaurant.

Page 190

B. Listen to the job interview. Circle *Yes* or *No*.

Luis: I'm applying for the job as a valet.
Manager: Do you have any experience?
Luis: No, but I was a cashier at Frank's Fried Chicken.
Manager: Do you have a clean driver's license? Any tickets?
Luis: My license is clean. No tickets. No accidents.
Manager: We need to check your driver's license. When can you start?
Luis: Tomorrow.
Manager: The job is part time. Wednesday and Thursday, 5:00 to 10:00. Friday, Saturday, and Sunday, we're very busy. The hours are 5:00 to 12:00. The pay is $3 an hour plus tips.
Luis: That's good.
Manager: Wear black slacks and black shoes. We'll give you a red jacket.
Luis: Thank you very much.

Page 192

The Big Picture: The Sunrise Hotel

A. Listen and circle.

My name is Ricardo Lopez. This is the Sunrise Hotel, and I'm the evening manager. The Sunrise Hotel is a big hotel, and it has more than 200 rooms. There's a restaurant, a bar, two swimming pools, and tennis courts. Many tourists like to stay here.

The hotel has about 100 employees. We have desk clerks, housekeepers, bellhops, landscapers, and restaurant employees. Then, we have a van driver. He drives the guests from the hotel to the airport.

We need people for all three shifts. People who work at night make one dollar more an hour than day employees. Some employees work full time, and we also have many part-time employees.

We are always looking for employees. The salary is low, and the employees work hard. Many employees leave us when they find a job with a better salary. But some people like the hours, and the workers like the tips. We have a friendly hotel here. Are you looking for a job? We have several job openings.

Page 193

B. Listen. Who is the manager speaking to?
1. Please clean rooms 371 and 374.
2. Could you park the cars for these guests, please?
3. Table 4 needs more water and the dessert menu.
4. How many empty rooms do we have for Saturday?
5. Some of these towels are not clean. What kind of detergent are you using?
6. The air conditioner isn't working in room 424. Could you check it?
7. Three guests need to get to the airport.

Unit 14: A Visit to the Doctor

Page 198 201

A. Listen and repeat.
1. Her head hurts.
2. Her back hurts.
3. Her stomach hurts.
4. His ear hurts.
5. His foot hurts.
6. His tooth hurts.

Page 203

A. Listen and repeat.
1. Use an ice pack.
2. Call the doctor.
3. Use an inhaler.
4. Put on lotion.
5. Take some aspirin.
6. Stay in bed.
7. Use a heating pad.
8. Drink liquids.

Page 208

The Big Picture: In the Waiting Room

A. Listen.
Dr. Johnson's waiting room is very busy. It's early spring, and many patients are sick. Mrs. Jacob is Dr. Johnson's nurse. She's talking to Mrs. Jackson. She's a new patient, so she's going to fill out a patient information form. Mrs. Lee is reading a magazine. She has a bad cough. The doctor is going to listen to her chest. Mr. Green is 75 years old, and he's in good health. He's in the office for his checkup. He has a checkup once a year. Mrs. Rios and her daughter, Julia, are in the office, too. Julia's crying because she has a bad burn on her finger. She burned her finger on the stove. Mr. Patel is holding his head. His head hurts. He has a bad headache. Miss Gonzales is sneezing and coughing. She has allergies, and she needs a prescription from Dr. Johnson. Mr. Henderson is talking to his son, Andy. Andy cut his arm and he needs a tetanus shot. He's scared because he doesn't like shots.

Unit 15: School

Page 214

A. Listen and complete.
1. Luisa **is playing** a game.
2. Cesar **is raising** his hand.
3. Yury **is drawing** a picture.
4. Irina and Marie **are reading** a story.
5. Paul and Michelle **are watching** a video.
6. Anita **is taking** a test.
7. Young Su **is working** in a group.

Page 219

C. Pronunciation: Ordinal numbers. Listen and repeat.

a. one	first	**e.** five	fifth	**i.** nine	ninth
b. two	second	**f.** six	sixth	**j.** ten	tenth
c. three	third	**g.** seven	seventh	**k.** eleven	eleventh
d. four	fourth	**h.** eight	eighth	**l.** twelve	twelfth

D. Listen and circle.

a. three	**d.** ten	**g.** eighth
b. twelfth	**e.** seventh	**h.** sixth
c. fourth	**f.** eleven	**i.** nine

E. Listen and circle.

1. seventh grade	**3.** tenth grade	**5.** eleventh grade
2. fourth grade	**4.** kindergarten	**6.** eighth grade

Page 220

A. Listen and complete.

1. Paula **doesn't raise** her hand to answer questions.
2. She **doesn't pay** attention.
3. She **doesn't get along** with her classmates.
4. She **doesn't do** her homework.
5. She **doesn't follow** directions.

Page 224

The Big Picture: In the Classroom

A. Listen.

This is Mr. Washington's fifth-grade social studies class. It is almost the end of the school year, so everyone is busy. Almost all of the students are working in groups. They are doing their final projects for the class. Ricky and Vicky are working on computers. Mr. Washington is helping them. Marta is also working on a computer. She has a question, so she is raising her hand. Ernest and Nancy are drawing a map. Gloria and Mei are cutting out pictures. Steve isn't sitting with a group because he doesn't like to work in groups. He likes to work alone. He is reading a book about science and writing a report. It is a very noisy classroom, but the students are working hard.

 Skills Index

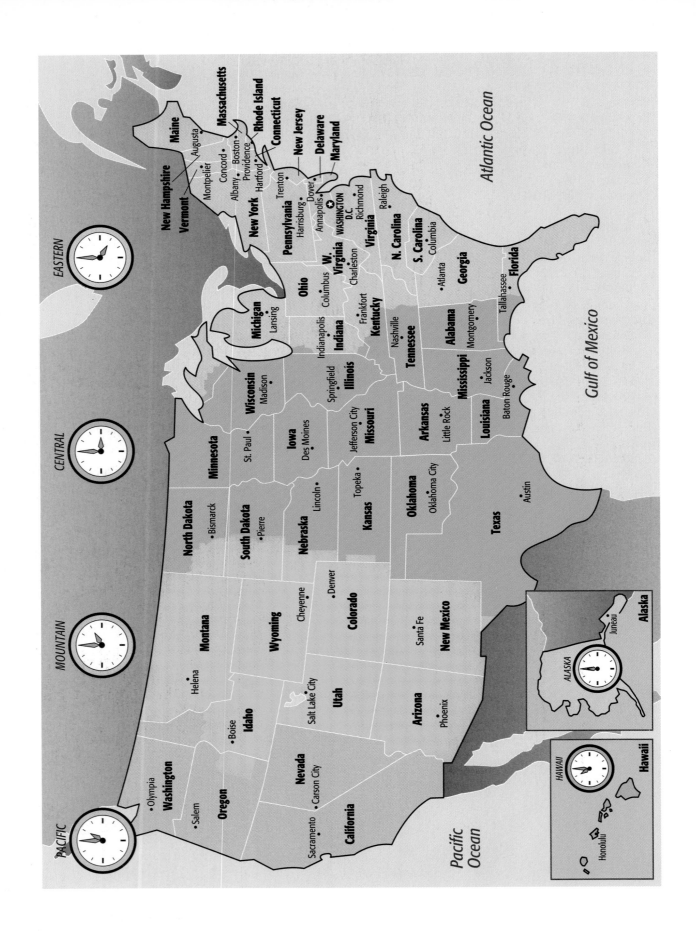